APOSTATE

FORREST REID

With wood engravings by
REYNOLDS STONE

faber and faber

This edition first published in 2011
by Faber and Faber Ltd
Bloomsbury House, 74–77 Great Russell Street
London WC1B 3DA

All rights reserved
© Queen's University of Belfast, 1926

The right of Forrest Reid to be identified as author of this work
has been asserted in accordance with Section 77 of the
Copyright, Designs and Patents Act 1988

This book is sold subject to the condition that it shall not, by way of
trade or otherwise, be lent, resold, hired out or otherwise circulated
without the publisher's prior consent in any form of binding or cover other than
that in which it is published and without a similar condition including this
condition being imposed on the subsequent purchaser

A CIP record for this book is available from the British Library

ISBN 978–0–571–28024–7

I

The primary impulse of the artist springs, I fancy, from discontent, and his art is a kind of crying for Elysium. In this single respect, perhaps, there is no difference between good and bad art. For in the most clumsy and bungled work (if it has been born of the desire for beauty) we should doubtless find, could we but pierce through the dead husk of it to the hidden conception, that same divine homesickness, that same longing for an Eden from which each one of us is exiled. Strangely different these paradisian visions. For me it may be the Islands of the Blest 'not shaken by winds nor ever wet with rain . . . where the clear air spreads without a cloud', for you the jewelled splendour of the New Jerusalem. Only in no case, I think, is it our own free creation. It is a country whose image was stamped upon our soul before we opened our eyes on earth, and all our life is little more than a trying to get back there, our art than a mapping of its mountains and streams.

I am speaking, of course, of a particular kind of art, for I know there are artists whose work bears witness to a complete acquiescence in the world and in life as it is. 'Fuir! là-bas fuir!'—it would be difficult to discover an echo of such a cry in any line written by Thackeray or Jane Austen. Take it, then, as a point of view suggested because it helps to explain my own writings, because the general impression remaining with me of the origin of these experiments and strivings is that they were for the most part prompted by just such a feeling of exile—exile from a world of which I did have a later glimpse from rare time to time. No matter how objective, how impersonal I tried to be, this subconscious lyrical emotion before long crept in, perhaps merely in a descriptive passage, in the dwelling upon this or that aspect or mood of nature, which had somehow opened a door into my secret world. Such an emotion runs all through the moon-story in *The Bracknels*, all through Grif's story in *The Spring Song*, and through much of Peter's in *Following Darkness*:[1] more, it is what constitutes the very atmosphere of these tales, which are most real just where they may appear to be most fantastic. And that is my only reason for mentioning them here—that and because they are, or were at the time, a part of my life. There is a sense in which it would be true to say that Denis and Grif and Peter are mere pretexts for the author to live again through the years of his boyhood, to live those years, as it were, more consciously, if less happily, though in each instance, except perhaps in that of Peter, nothing could have been farther from his intention than an essay in self-portraiture. These dream-children, indeed, differ from one another as widely as members of a single family can do. And if I were to add to them other youngsters from other tales, down to the nameless young criminal of *The Accomplice*, even the family resemblance would, I think, die out. Yet all have one thing in common, all of them are, in a sense, seen by the story-teller moving under the skies of his own particular dream world, breathing its air, standing on the shore of its familiar sea. They have come from that world, they are its inhabitants, they are not invented; but, clothed and complete in every detail, they walked into his room, without invitation, without apology.

It is difficult, therefore, to understand why, when for once the historian sets out deliberately on a voyage of rediscovery, the way should suddenly reveal itself as beset with pitfalls, and even the prime actor in the tale should have taken fright and withdrawn himself into a hiding-place. It is as if we actually could get closer to truth through fiction than through fact. It is not only the natural fear of creating an impression of offensive egotism which proves hampering; there is the further drawback that, while the imaginary world we create when writing a story lies unveiled before us, Time, I find, has dropped veil beyond veil between me and the real world

[1] Rewritten as *Peter Waring*.

I am trying to evoke. I may promise to present it and the people who lived in it without a rag of disguise, but I know I cannot keep my promise.

When I was about six or seven I used to be taken out each morning by my nurse, Emma, to the Botanic Gardens, at that time not yet transformed into a public park. There was a large conservatory there, and the wing of the building where the palms and cactus grew had a glass door bordered with red and yellow panes. On chilly October days I was very fond of flattening my nose against one of these coloured windows, and peering out into an exotic world. What I saw then, in spite of the familiar shape and position of each tree and shrub, was not the Botanic Gardens at all, but a tropical landscape, luxuriant and gorgeous. The damp warmth of the greenhouse atmosphere, the moist earthy smell of the ferns and creepers and mosses growing there, helped to deepen the illusion that I was far away in the virgin forest. Tigers and panthers burned in those shrubberies, and scarlet, green, and blue parrots screamed soundlessly in the trees. Soundlessly as yet; and as yet the tigers skulked almost unseen; but in a very few minutes I knew I should pass really into their country. These minutes, unfortunately, I was never granted; I had not been brought out to spend my morning in an overheated conservatory which gave Emma a headache; and though I did not yield without demur, in the twinkling of an eye I would find myself back again in grey October and the unromantic Gardens, where perambulators rolled leisurely, and everything was dull and domestic.

Looking back through Time is very much the same as looking through that greenhouse door. The shapes of things remain unaltered, but there is a soft colour floating about them that did not exist in the clear white light of morning. Only, again, I am not sure—am not sure, I mean, that this clear white light ever did exist for me. I cannot help thinking that I was in those days very much what I am now. My life, from as far back as I can remember, was never lived wholly in the open. I mean that it had its private side, that there were things I saw, felt, heard, and kept to myself. There were thoughts I kept to myself, too; and above all dreams. Not deliberately, I dare say, but because I had not yet words in which to put them. If you stand quite still in an ancient house, you will hear, even in broad daylight, strange sounds and murmurings. And so it was with me. I came, on my mother's side, of a very old, perhaps too old a stock, one that had reached its prime four hundred years ago, and there were whisperings and promptings which when I was quite alone reached me out of the past. Very early I perceived that one's mind was swarming with ghosts; very early I became convinced that one had thoughts that were not one's own thoughts, that one remembered things one had never been told (certainly not by Emma); and these thoughts and memories one could not speak of—not here, not now—though one could speak of them in the dream place. Only, there I did not need to speak of them: there, somehow, they were no longer thoughts, but things that happened—beautifully, wonderfully—so that I could have cried on awaking.

II

There are certain things I cannot remember learning, though I can remember very well when I did not know them. I cannot remember learning to read, for instance, but I can remember learning to count, because of the astonishing behaviour of Thirteen. Thirteen refused to pass my lips, so that I was obliged to skip from twelve to fourteen, while knowing all the time there was a nameless lurker skulking somewhere in the darkness. I would make an angry grab at him, but always he eluded me, and 'Fourteen, fourteen' would be offered to the critical Emma as my nearest approach to the desired sequence. Yet I go back, I suppose, even further than this in recalling a period when my own people were strangers to me (my father, mother, and elder brothers and sisters), when I was uneasy in their presence, as in the presence of the unknown, when everything indeed, so far as I was concerned, began and ended with Emma.

It must have been several years later, it must have been after his death and after the disappearance of Emma from my life, when I learned such few facts as I did learn about my father. These facts I may as well put down here. His name was Robert. The first Forrest Reid was born in 1751, and had a family of seventeen children. He was the grandson of a John Reid who had been exiled with other Presbyterians to the Bass Rock during the religious persecutions of the reign of Charles II, and from the Rock had been shipped to Jamaica. It was the son of John Reid who in 1745 married Margaret, eldest daughter of James Forrest, thus bringing the name as a Christian name into our family. Middle-class, Presbyterian folk all of them, living round and about Lurgan and Derry, though my father himself had left Ireland when he was a young man. But I made no enquiries into these matters, and I give now only what I picked up casually as a child. I know that when, in 1859, a few years after the death of his first wife, my father married again, he was a shipowner in Liverpool, his partner being Captain Washington Pirrie, after whom one of my brothers was called; and I know that some time later an attempt to run the blockade during the American War ended disastrously. I have heard from my mother an account of the night when the bad news arrived. It had been a gamble; all had been staked, and all was lost. But to me it was quite unimportant; it had happened years before I was born, nor did I realize that my own surroundings would have been very different on that day had the dice fallen luckily. The result, at any rate, was that my father's house and furniture and collection of pictures were sold, and that he himself was obliged to return to Ireland and begin all over again in Belfast, this time in a subordinate position, as manager of Anderson's Felt Works. On his arrival in Ireland he took the house that was formerly the Club House of the Royal Ulster Yacht Club at Bangor, county Down; from there he removed to Windsor Avenue, Belfast, and finally to 20 Mount Charles, where I was born, some five or six years before his death.

I confess I have but the vaguest memory of my father, though in five years, even if they happen to be one's first, there is surely time to receive a definite impression. But I received none. Probably my rather tardy arrival (considerably after twelve predecessors, only six of whom had survived) found him a little blasé where children were concerned, and if, in the evening, after dinner, I was occasionally brought down for a few minutes, that represents the full extent of our acquaintance. There lies before me as I write a small photograph showing him standing at a davenport, a French newspaper, the title of which I cannot make out, in his hands. He is dressed in a long dark coat and light-grey trousers. He has a wide collar of the kind to be seen in portraits of Mr. Gladstone, and his tie is tied in a broad bow. His hair is thick and wavy; he wears spectacles, and is clean shaven except for short side whiskers of the kind called 'mutton-chop'. He looks mild and old-fashioned, and at the back of the faded carte-de-visite there is sprawled in my own handwriting—oddly recognizable still—the word 'Farther'. Nevertheless, the picture, with its inscription, suggests nothing to me now beyond the fact that I must have 'collected' photographs at some early date. I cannot even fit it into my shadowy impression of those occasional appearances at dessert, when he would offer me half-crowns, and even half-sovereigns, largely, I imagine, for the amusement of watching Emma's fruitless attempts to make me accept them. I knew nothing of the purchasing power of money, but I knew that its appearance was extremely disagreeable to me, as was the appearance of shining buttons, seals, rings, etc. I would as soon have lifted a cockroach in my hand as have touched one of those glistening coins.

III

Emma had nursed us all, but none of the others had been so exclusively her property as I was. This arrangement suited me admirably, for I had conceived for her an affection which neither my mother nor anybody else in later life was to oust. Emma came first, and she remained first. In those days I don't suppose I thought about her at all: she was simply there, an essential part of my existence, like the air I breathed or the sun that warmed me. She was even mentioned after everybody else in my 'prayers'—that old parrot song she had taught me, and which, from her knee, I nightly offered up to a deity more drowsy than myself. Certainly her care for me was far beyond any that deities are wont to practise. It had a beautiful quality of mingled tenderness and wisdom, so that I cannot remember the slightest cloud darkening the happiness of those earliest years.

A brother and a sister shared to some extent the day nursery with me, but they were my seniors by several years, and hardly counted in my scheme of things. Of far more immediate interest was the personality of a sagacious old tabby, who would stroll into the nursery and lie on the floor in the sun, and was good-natured enough to purr when I used her as a pillow. I was aware that she timed these visits, and that if she did not find me alone (by which I mean alone with Emma) she would not stay. Not that she was, so far as I recall, a particularly affectionate animal. Cats are never sentimental; they treat you exactly as you treat them; and it was simply that she had marked me down, with unerring instinct, as 'safe'—a person who could be trusted to amuse the kittens while one dozed and dreamed.

Nearly all animals possess this instinct, this gift of divining an innate sympathy or its opposite. I have heard a benevolent old dog growl at the approach of some toddler of three, and have known he had a reason for doing so which bore no resemblance to that suggested either by his astonished master or the indignant parents of the child. Such a sympathy, indeed, can never be acquired; it has nothing to do with a habit of treating animals fairly, which *can* be acquired; it is a thing implanted at birth, a temperamental bias. It was just this bias, I dare say (to take a very ancient instance), which gave its peculiar form to the teaching of Empedocles, and lay behind all that philosopher's hatred of blood sacrifice and of the eating of flesh. In my own case it was broad enough to include even the battered stone lions in University Square, creatures I fed daily in my morning walks. Later on, my mother discouraged this sympathy, believing it exaggerated. She would not allow me to keep a dog, and even a cat was only tolerated because cats were preferable to mice. She herself had no liking for animals. They were all right in their proper place, and of course one must not ill-treat them, but their proper place, I gathered, was at a considerable distance from our house. Emma, though for all I know to the contrary she too may have been indifferent to animals, as usual understood; and so each morning we sallied out with our little parcel of provisions.

And thus I seem to see, as if at the end of an immense vista, these two figures moving sedately through the sunshine, the smaller with his hands clasped behind his back, a habit he clung to even when running. He is dressed each day in a fresh blue or brown or white or even pink sailor suit, and on his head a wide-brimmed straw hat is held firmly by an elastic band that passes under his chin. Beside this figure walks (though never holding his hand) the figure of Emma, clad in a long dark green double-breasted coat, and carrying in one black-gloved hand a parcel of bread, and in the other an umbrella. Their destination is the Botanic Gardens *via* University Square and the stone lions, and when they reach the Gardens they keep severely to themselves. Emma never talks to the other nurses, the little boy never talks to the other little boys. They may stop for a minute or two if they should chance to meet lovely Mrs. Gerrard or some other of mamma's friends, and the beauty of Mrs. Gerrard alone among these friends, the sweetness of her smile, and the soft southern music of her voice, awaken deep down in the little boy a curious thrill. She, too, somehow belongs to his happy world —that most bizarre garden of Epicurus, which includes the Wesleyan Emma, and three such frank pagans as Mrs. Gerrard, tabby, and himself. I don't know that I am very successfully concealing the fact that I have a weakness for this little boy. He is shy, and at times, it may be, a little odd in his behaviour, but I cannot help thinking him a not unpleasant person. It is indeed a pity this chronicle should have to take note shortly of a rapid deterioration which set in during the years after Emma had gone home to England— years through which the words 'that odious child!' seem to me now to sound like a perpetual refrain. The words reach me, it is true, always in the voice of my eldest sister, but even comparative strangers recognized their aptness—recognized, at all events, to whom they referred.

IV

That Emma precisely resembled the Emma I now see when thinking of her is more than doubtful. I was a boy of six when she left us, and a child's vision of grown-up people is true perhaps at any time only for other children. As I recall her, she is ageless: she is neither stout nor thin, neither tall nor short, her eyes are grey, her complexion fair. Her hair, just a shade too dark to be called flaxen, must, I think, have been worn drawn up over a pad, because one of these discarded pads became my nightly bedfellow till it was superseded by a stuffed brown velvet elephant, a beast whom I loved less than Dobbin, a battered old wooden horse, but who was more comfortable to hug against one's stomach.

Emma was English; her full name was Emma Holmes; and her native town was Bootle—a town I privately decided to be unattractive. For in my mind's eye I had a picture of Bootle, drab and populous, a place of endless streets in which every other house was a shop. Bootle!—its very name described it. And the nieces lived at Bootle—Emma's nieces—of whom she occasionally spoke. I had formed a picture of the nieces also, unflattering, unwarrantable. But the eldest was engaged to a young man in a shop, and that in itself, to my snobbish little soul, was sufficient. I saw the nieces as all fluffy fair hair and giggles, and even the assurance that I came before them in Emma's affections failed to soften my heart. For the nieces, I determined, Bootle was just the place. They lived there—largely upon shrimps—and these mysterious crustacea created indeed a kind of bond between them and Emma. Secretly, while affecting indifference and a vague superiority, I was much worried by the thought of shrimps. I could form no conception even of what the delicious things looked like. Apparently they were peculiar to Bootle, where other dainties also abounded—pig's feet, and tripe—none of which I had so much as seen, let alone tasted. On Emma's birthdays little white netted doilies would arrive (from the nieces), and these I learned were intended for shrimp-pots. But as the shrimps themselves never accompanied the doilies my ignorance remained unenlightened. The doilies were merely wrapped up again in their tissue paper and put away in that large bottom drawer of Emma's wardrobe whither all presents eventually passed. A gift, to her, was a sacred thing, to be laid by in lavender—or, perhaps more accurately, camphor—out of the reach of moth and dust. All my own silly little gifts, however obviously intended for daily use, found their way after a week or so to the bottom drawer. Sometimes, indeed, she had to take them out again, because I wanted to see them. Then she would place them on the four-poster that stood beside my smaller bed, while I hopped round and round admiring the spectacle of my own generosity. But I never asked for a second look at the doilies.

Emma was deeply religious, and she is the only deeply religious person I have met with whom I have been able to feel quite happy and at my ease. Doubtless her creed was narrow, and probably it was gloomy; but she herself was so emphatically *not* narrow and *not* gloomy that it mattered very little what she supposed herself to believe. I dare say it was part of her creed that it was sinful for little boys to play games on Sundays; nevertheless, every Sunday I played perfectly happily on the floor at her feet, while she nodded in her rocking-chair over the big Bible that had a picture of John Wesley on the front page. Doubtless it was part of her creed that little boys should be taken to chapel; but after a single experiment, during which I expressed my permanent 'reaction' to Christianity by howling like a small bull with rage and boredom, chapel was abandoned. It was the only naughtiness I can remember having been guilty of during her rule, and the whole thing took me so completely unawares that I still think there was an excuse for it. Chapel I had pictured as an entertaining place, since Emma was so fond of it, therefore my surprise and indignation when the reality was revealed to me may be imagined. I felt that I had been deceived; and by Emma of all people. Why should I have been brought among these dismal, noisy persons? Why should I be kept perched on a high uncomfortable wooden bench in an ugly crowded building when, after five minutes of it, I had expressed an urgent desire to go home? Emma, indeed, brought me home shortly afterwards, but not before I had raised my voice in weeping, and kicked the pew in front of me, and thrown a hymn-book on the floor. She did not scold me when we got outside, she simply explained that I should like chapel when I grew older, a prophecy which, in the event, failed to prove true.

After her departure, which took place not many months later, Sunday became to me a veritable nightmare, casting its baleful shadow even over the last hours of Saturday. I hated Sunday, I hated church, I hated Sunday School, I hated Bible stories, I hated everybody mentioned in both the Old and New Testaments, except perhaps the impenitent thief, Eve's snake, and a few similar characters. And I never disguised these feelings. From dawn till sunset the day of rest was for me a day of storm and battle, renewed each week, and carried on for years with a pertinacity that now seems hardly credible, till at length the opposition was exhausted and I was allowed to go my own way. With Emma there could never have been such scenes. Her infinite tolerance and understanding would have made them impossible. Her deep desire was that one should be good, but her still deeper desire was that one should be happy; and she would never have believed it good to go to church with a heart of fury, a face like a thunder-cloud, and a fixed determination to do, out of revenge, whatsoever was *not* pleasing in the sight of the Lord.

Yet nothing could be farther from the truth than that she simply allowed me to take my own way. I myself, indeed, unless my way had been her way, should have got little pleasure from it. Her rule was supreme, but it was an influence, not a rigid law; it was something of which at the time one was not conscious; and though an old white satin ball-slipper was kept (a little incongruously) for purposes of chastisement, it was merely a symbol, it had never been used, and was indeed the subject of some of our earliest jokes. The whole secret is that Emma was wise, and the rule of the wise is never oppressive, never violent or retributive or lachrymose. It establishes a sense of companionship and security, a comforting feeling—comforting particularly to an imaginative child—that there is someone who will always understand, and therefore always be just. And justice is the quality a child values above everything. Not all the capricious affection in the world will make up to him for its absence. When it fails, he is wounded, so that the wound leaves a scar. But the sickly, the neurotic, the unhappy, the narrowly religious —how can they be just? Association with such persons has a malign effect upon a child, and the more sensitive and intelligent he is the worse that effect will be. Emma, it is true, was a Christian, but somehow her Christianity never interfered with my sense of freedom. Doubtless it was there as a background, a kind of atmosphere, but an atmosphere so soft and sunny that the tenderest young pagan plants might have grown up and expanded happily within it. Thus it came about that my only experience of chapel left no cloud in the sky. On the afternoon of that same Sunday I built my towered cities (I had inherited baskets-full of bricks) on the nursery floor in perfect contentment, while she sat with her back to the window, in the big rocking-chair that later became my own, reading *Good Words* or *The Quiver* (we took in these magazines together with the more secular *Argosy* and *Chambers's Journal*), or possibly her Wesley Bible, in which she had marked off beautifully in her pointed delicate handwriting the texts of all the sermons she had heard, with the dates, and the names of the preachers. (That Bible, too, she left behind for me.)

My cities were Greece, Athens, and the Peloponnesian States, and they were peopled by a military crowd, for there had come down to me from older brothers many armies of leaden soldiers. But where the names of my cities came from I have not a notion. I only know that these cities were perpetually at war, and that the war was carried on by throwing a solid square of india rubber, myself being marksman, and each city having its shot in turn. The nursery was a large bare oil-clothed room with a bow window, and my cities were built against three of its walls. How gloriously those towers and battlements and gates came crashing down! And the struggle was carried on to a bloody finish, till only one man would be left standing, a lonely conqueror amid all the rack and ruin.

It was a good sport; I could enjoy it very well at this moment, for my tastes have not greatly changed. It would have been better had I had a companion or two, but unless Charlie, who alone of my brothers was still a schoolboy, cared to join in, there was nobody. And Charlie did not often join in. I was too small, I suppose; he had his own friends; and at any rate our temperaments were singularly incompatible.

At this time I had not yet learned to read, and though I had a few picture-books I seldom looked at them. The largest, indeed, I never opened at all. It was Lear's *Book of Nonsense*, and the grotesque drawings, so far from amusing me, aroused a feeling of repulsion and uneasiness. I could not have told you why I found them repellent. The words 'deformed', 'abnormal', were not in my vocabulary. I should probably have called the pictures ugly, but in doing so should not in the least have expressed what I meant. A tale of Hoffmann's (which must have been read to me several years later) produced a precisely similar effect. Lear's drawings, Hoffmann's story, seemed to me not imaginative, but to belong to a very real and horrible world whose fringes I had once or twice touched in dreams.

Sometimes Emma told me stories of her own, and sometimes she read to me, and sometimes she told me poetry—old, old rhymes, such as the following. I have got some of the words wrong, I know, but as this is how they then went in my mind I shall not change them.

> *Indeed, indeed, in double deed,*
> *I sowed a garden full of seed,*
>
> *And when the seed began to grow*
> *'Twas like a garden full of snow,*
>
> *And when the snow began to melt*
> *'Twas like a ship without a belt,*
>
> *And when the ship began to sail*
> *'Twas like a bird without a tail,*
>
> *And when the bird began to fly*
> *'Twas like a needle in the sky,*
>
> *And when the sky began to roar*
> *'Twas like a lion at the door,*
>
> *And when the door began to crack*
> *'Twas like a stick upon my back,*
>
> *And when my back began to smart*
> *'Twas like a penknife in my heart,*
>
> *But when my heart began to bleed*
> *'Twas time for me to die indeed.*

This poem possessed for me a peculiar fascination, though I knew no more what it *meant* than I now know what Blake's *Crystal Cabinet* means. I liked it simply because it called up a series of tragic pictures. I saw the bare wintry garden, with a few blackened stalks and branches rising above a waste of snow. Below the garden a stormy sea broke on a desolate beach, and far out on that grey sea a bare black hulk, a mere shell, rose and dipped sullenly against the lowering sky. As for the gigantic 'needle' which stretched right across the heavens, the word, now that I come to write it down, must I feel sure be wrong. Emma must have said 'eagle', unless the mistake goes still farther back, to the days of her own childhood. Be that as it may, the lines shaped for me a dream story—one of those stories whose lack of logic, whose cracks and crevices, the imagination covers like a luxuriant creeper. 'How many miles to Babylon?'—that was another, more visionary poem. And the first stanza of this:

> *I saw three ships come sailing by,*
> *Come sailing by, come sailing by;*
> *I saw three ships come sailing by*
> *On Christmas day in the morning.*

Later there was a delightful, long poem, learned by my sister Fanny at Mrs. Byers's school, as an 'action song', which went to so swinging a tune that one could not help adding one's own shrill pipe to the chorus.

> *A fox jumped up in a hungry plight*
> *And begged the moon to give him light,*
> *For he'd many miles to trot that night*
> *Before he reached his den, O!*
>   *Den, O! Den, O!*
> *For he'd many miles to trot that night*
> *Before he reached his den, O!*
>
>   *   *   *
>
> *He took the grey goose by the neck*
> *And slung her up across his back,*
> *The black duck cried out 'Quack! quack! quack!'*
> *But the fox is off to his den, O!*
>   *Den, O! Den, O!*
> *The black duck cried out 'Quack! quack! quack!'*
> *But the fox is off to his den, O!*
>
> *Old mother Slipper Slapper jumped out of bed,*
> *And out of the window popped her head,*
> *'O John! John! John! the grey goose is gone,*
> *And the fox is off to his den, O!*
>   *Den, O! Den, O!*
> *O John! John! John! the grey goose is gone,*
> *And the fox is off to his den, O!'*

But I have forgotten most of the verses, and even those leading up to the tremendous finale shouted with all the power of one's lungs: 'And the little ones picked the bones, O!'

No fairy stories came my way, so I suppose Emma did not care for them. Nor were there, now that I think of it, ever any ogres or giants or talking beasts or witches in her own tales, which she produced with the ease and copiousness of an Anthony Trollope. These were, in fact, realistic in tone, dealing with the everyday adventures and misadventures of small boys, whose divagations from the path of virtue met with no severer punishments than they would have in actual life. And the settings of these stories were so detailed, down to the very patterns on the carpets and wallpapers, that I more than half believed them true. The heroes I envied principally for the reason that they were possessed of real suits of clothes, with proper jackets and knickerbockers, not silly sailor things whose trousers were shaped like baggy bathing-drawers and had no pockets. Persistently I enquired about their clothes, with the consequence that, though their wardrobes were already crowded to bursting point, they were constantly paying further visits to their tailors. I liked these stories; they amused me vastly. It was one of their charms that I myself could ever give a fresh turn to the plot by a timely question, and another that they could be carried on indefinitely. They brightened our walks on the dullest days; new characters were for ever appearing in them, whose very names would make me die of laughing. Nevertheless, it was not till, all unknown to me, the days of our companionship were already numbered, that *my* kind of story, the kind of story I seemed somehow to remember, to recognize, to have once lived in, was suddenly revealed. All the other tales had belonged to a world outside me; here was one belonging to my very own world, my private world, of which I had never breathed a syllable to a living soul. Emma had begun to take in a little magazine (I think it appeared weekly) called *Early Days*, and the serial story in it she read aloud to me. I fancy, now, *Early Days* must have been taken especially for me. It was a journal intended for Sunday reading, a sort of juvenile *Quiver*, and my story very likely was an allegory composed with the definite purpose of awakening pious longings in the breasts of its young readers. That distant, mysterious island, whose mountain peaks, when the setting sun caught them, could just be made out, far across the sea, by the children gathered on the shore—was it not heaven? That blue, sleepy sea, breaking monotonously on a coral beach—was it not life? Those children, setting sail one by one in search of El Dorado—were they not little pilgrims, little nephews of Christian and Christiana? I think so. But in that case, with one reader (or listener) I can vouch for it the author missed his mark. His story was for me, thirteen years before I saw them, simply Watteau's *Embarquement pour Cythère*, and Giorgione's *Venetian Pastoral*—an augury of my own nocturnal voyages, which had not yet, so far as I knew, properly begun. The scene was there before me, strangely familiar, as if I were retracing my own footmarks in the sand. Not that it was described in the actual tale. It was only that I saw—saw while Emma read—the dark summer sea widening out and out till it melted into a golden haze that hid yet suggested an enchanted land beyond. The light turned to bright burnished gold where it caught the top of a remote mountain, but here, close at hand, in the rich deep drowsy afternoon, was a smooth green lawn dropping down gently to a white sandy bay where dark waves toppled over in foam and music. Here was a bright delicate company, young, beautiful, gay, yet 'sad with the whole of pleasure'. Here were the brown faces, the pouting lips and naked unspoiled bodies, the slim Pan pipes, the shadowed grass.

> *Now the hand trails upon the viol string*
> *That sobs, and the brown faces cease to sing....*

'My world! My world!' I could have shouted; and though Emma might have answered, 'Not there, not there, my child,' I should have known better. There—there—or nowhere. It was the only heaven I wanted, or ever was to want. Fleeting glimpses I have had of it, and lost them: and from the flame of that vision I have awakened desolate and sick with longing. For the life I came back to seemed pale and feeble as a candle in the blazing sun; and the knowledge that the other was there—there in all its splendour and beauty and completeness—if only I could reach it, turned all ordinary ambitions and interests to a kind of languor.

> *The sunset is not yet, the dawn is gone;*
> *Yet in our eyes the light hath paled and passed;*
> *But twilight shall be lovely as the dawn,*
> *And night shall bring forgetfulness at last.*

It is not true: twilight can never be lovely as the dawn: its beauty is an opiate beauty that is half sleep and half resignation, and wholly melancholy. It may bring peace, but what is peace compared with joy? Even the memory of a single rapturous hour is better than years passed in untroubled shadow. The endless night with its forgetfulness has closed upon Emma. She never finished that story to me. She left before it had quite run its course, and though she sent me the completed magazine, all vivid and splendid in a gilt and scarlet binding, I never finished it myself. I did not know she was going. I knew nothing when I fell asleep that night. It had all been kept a foolish secret from me, though not, I am sure, at her desire. Was she to have left me, then, without saying good-bye? I do not know even that. But if such were the plan, her resolution must at the last have failed her. I was wakened up. I remember kneeling on the bed in my nightshirt, bewildered, blinking, my arms round her neck. She was dressed, she had her hat on, she was all ready to go, the cab was waiting in the street, her luggage had been carried downstairs. I could not understand. She had gone away before—gone for a week or a fortnight to the nieces in Bootle —but it had been quite different from this: there had been no waking at night, there had been the assurance that she was coming back. This time she was not to come back. She did not deceive me with a false promise. Somebody called from down below. My arms were clinging round her: and then I was alone. . . .

I do not remember whether my mother came to me or not. If she did, I did not want her. I remember nothing after that parting. A cloud, utterly impenetrable, has descended upon the hours and days and weeks and months and even years that followed: when it lifts I am a quite different person, the transition from childhood to boyhood has been completed—somehow, somewhere, in the darkness—but of the process and all that accompanied it I can recall absolutely nothing.

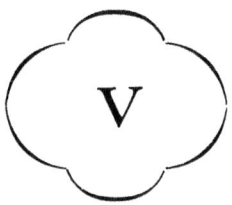

V

No other course is open to me than to jump the next two or three years, so that I may alight on a safer ground than that of mere conjecture. I seem suddenly to have become dull, incapable of receiving new impressions, or, at any rate, of retaining them. Stir as I may in the well of memory, nothing whatever rises to the surface. And yet the changes in my life at this time must have been abrupt and radical. I must, for instance, on the morning after that memorable night, have come down for the first time to breakfast with the rest of the family; I must henceforth have taken up my part in the common existence:—not a shadow of it all remains with me now. Apparently I was 'good'; by which I mean sufficiently stupefied not to have dreamed of asking questions. I did not ask why Emma had gone—nor did anybody tell me. I did not express grief at her departure. Indeed, I never alluded to the matter at all, either then or later. My fount of life, of interest, of curiosity, was temporarily dried up, so that when we moved from number 20 to number 15 Mount Charles, a smaller, cheaper house on the opposite and shady side of the street, this adventure, too, passed as if it had been accomplished in my sleep. The only thing that vaguely reaches me from that shrouded, chrysalid interval (and probably marks the closing of it), is a sense of struggle against something that was at the time heavy and oppressive, but which now, on examination, shrinks to the mere enforced companionship of the youngest of my sisters. The contrast with the past was, I suppose, too extreme not to awaken even in my apathetic soul a sullen hatred of it. It meant that, though I was really alone, I was not allowed to be alone.

The arrangement, certainly, was not ideal; this sister,

Connie, six years older than myself, being just of an age for which my own age was the wrong one. My presence was bound to be a source of annoyance to her, and she exerted her authority the more despotically on that account. She had two bosom friends, school friends, and I, dragging reluctantly behind them, resentful and defiant, was naturally an unmitigated nuisance. Instead of being at liberty to do what they liked, they now had the daily task of looking after me. Not that for a moment this was allowed to interrupt the buzz of conversation, unflagging as that of Selina and the Vicarage girls, which from start to finish of our dreary walks was the sole entertainment provided. Not one of the three ever addressed a word to me except of an admonitory nature, nor was the slightest notice taken of my own few remarks. And if a picnic, a hunt for primroses or blackberries, or anything really enjoyable, were afoot, I was invariably left behind on the plea that the place selected would be beyond my walking powers. The solicitude expressed for me at such times was touching. Thanks to it, I was not included in the river parties, was not included in the skating parties to Ballydrain, was not included in anything except dismal walks up the Malone Road and down again. No greater fallacy exists than that the youngest of a large family has the best time. He hasn't. He is out of it from the start. Wherever he turns he is met by the signs of prior claims. He is like a person who enters a crowded railway-carriage; the only thing for him to do is to assume as bold an air as possible and make use of his small elbows. I much preferred being taken out by my older sisters, because they had an engaging fashion of pretending I was their grandfather. This was amusing, but it happened all too rarely: to Connie—as a kind of millstone round her neck—I was attached permanently, until the time came when I might go my own ways and make my own friends. The curious thing is that, though she did not want me, and I asked for nothing better than to be left behind, if ever I attempted to escape she would pursue me like an avenging angel, and not only capture me, but unfailingly report my conduct at home. Flight was indeed useless, my short legs were no match for her long ones, and even if they had been, the younger of the two friends was a very Atalanta for swiftness of foot. Once more within their grasp, the conversation would be resumed in its deadly clack, clack, clack, with an occasional whispering designed to exclude me still further, but which merely aroused my wandering attention. Yet, through it all, some kind of secret and rather rapid development must have been taking place, for when, at the end of this foggy period, the light once more breaks, my clouds of glory are perceptibly a little tarnished, my feet are set definitely upon the path they are henceforth to follow, I am equipped with a precocious, if fragmentary knowledge of life, and Emma, and my life with Emma, seem as remote as that distant island of which we had once read.

My freedom came to me, I suppose, when I was between eight and nine. I now was allowed to play with other boys, companions of my own choosing, though my mother, by some strange fatality, never approved of those I did choose.

No such intimate relations existed between my mother and me as had existed between me and Emma. Nor was this chiefly, or even at all, I think, because Emma had come first. It was not because she had come first that she was inseparably united in my mind with all that was supremely lovable, all that still dropped softly back into one's spirit when one was alone. There was in Emma's nature something I had dimly felt to be deep and unchangeable, there was an infinite pleasantness that had touched each humdrum detail in the small routine of my life with happiness and beauty, so that even getting up and dressing on a cold winter morning became a kind of game. All that was gone. I accommodated myself to the change, but it never occurred to me that my mother might take the place of my first love. Perhaps there were too many of us, too many claims upon her affection, so that, divided and somewhat preoccupied, it seemed a little thin and chilly in comparison with what had been taken from me. Yet my mother was completely unselfish—unselfish where her children were concerned. It may therefore be that a little boy for whom this was not sufficient was both ungrateful and hard-hearted. I can say no more than that it *was* not sufficient—not sufficient to break down the wall of reserve which, since Emma's departure, had been built up round my soul. Nobody, I hasten to add, ever showed a desire to break down that wall: nobody, to be quite truthful, was even aware of its existence. My mother was simple, literal; she had very little imagination, and no sense of humour. What it really amounts to, I dare say, was that I had grown accustomed to, and learned to love, something that was in its essence different from anything she could give me. I had grown accustomed to having my thoughts divined, my groping unsuccessful words understood, my body and my spirit strengthened and nurtured in the bosom of a profound and watchful tenderness. The word 'bosom', which I wrote unconsciously, has really in this place a definite significance. For there was something in that tenderness, its strong, protective, life-giving quality, which to-day invariably associates itself in my mind with the old Greek tale of the wandering Demeter, who comes to the farm house (in Ovid's version of the story), and nurses the mortal child Demophon, placing him nightly in the red heart of the fire, that she may burn out of him what is gross and weak. And as that work was interrupted by the prying fears of a fond and foolish mother, so too was this other work, though for a different reason.

But such reveries are fanciful, flattering at the same time to myself. The proper subject of this chapter is my mother. I know I must have given an impression of a lack of sympathy between us, and I should like to tone that impression down. It is indeed, in such matters, extraordinarily difficult to find words to express the exact shade of one's meaning. A lack of sympathy, I fear, did exist, but it was not an active quantity, nor one that came into play in the superficial affairs of everyday life: my mother, for instance, I am sure, was entirely unconscious of it. And here, in fact, one aspect of it seems to be revealed. I mean, she was conscious of so little that had to do with my private life, my life as an individual, as distinct from the common life of the hive. Our relations were affectionate, but they were never intimate, never confidential. The fault may have been my own, but I am inclined to believe it was nobody's. It was as if, deep down below the surface, something within me, reaching out tentatively, was met by a blank wall of insensibility. And there was even more than that; there was something that had power to inflict a wound, that had inflicted more than one wound; and, because of an insidious poison in them, these wounds did not heal, they rankled and secreted a corrosive element that remained, that remained all the more obstinately because for long periods it would lie dormant and forgotten. It is there still.

I remember, for example, being punished for remarking that Mr. MacIlwaine would not pull down his blinds tonight. Mr. MacIlwaine was an old gentleman who lived in the house opposite ours (our own old house, in fact), and every evening I used to watch him light his gas, and stand for a moment or two at the window looking out into the darkness (rather sadly, and yet pleasantly, I thought) before he lowered the Venetian blinds. But on the evening of my luckless speech the blinds were already down, had been down all day, because Mr. MacIlwaine, as I and everybody else knew, lay dead in one of the upper rooms. I had not the slightest intention of showing disrespect to him; I was not indifferent to him, as my mother really was—I liked him, liked him in the way I sometimes got to like people to whom I had never spoken a word; my remark was thrown off innocently, just as the thought had risen in my mind; but it stirred some deep and unaccountable spring of irritation in my mother, and it was as if I had violated a tomb. The suddenness of her anger, like an unexpected blow in the face, did not make me feel I had done wrong: it merely bewildered me and aroused my own anger. The circumstance was slight—a misunderstanding, shall we say?—but it was one of a series, a series which had in the end the result of making me extremely uncommunicative. In the old days there had been no misunderstandings.

My mother was English through and through. Also, unlike my father, who came of plain middle-class stock, she was an aristocrat. Her own name was there for me to read in Burke, the Burke of 1863 (coming almost at the end of the article headed 'Parr of Parr'), with the whole history of her forbears right on back to the eleventh century, a great family even then, though it has since, in the direct line, died out. I would pause over the more spectacular names: William Parr, Earl of Essex and Marquess of Northampton; Anne Parr, married to William Herbert, Earl of Pembroke (grandfather of Shakespeare's Mr. W. H.); Katherine Parr, last and most fortunate of the wives of Henry VIII. It pleased me, I confess, to find my own mother in a book, and the fact that none of her people had shown the slightest interest in us, that I had never set eyes even on my grandmother, that neither she, nor any of my mother's sisters—Aunt Katherine, Aunt Blanche, Aunt Alice, Aunt Connie, Aunt Helena—had ever so much as crossed the doors of our house or invited us to cross their doors, did not at that time strike me as it would strike me now. It seemed perfectly natural that I should have a lot of relations—grandmother, aunts, cousins—whom I had never seen, and they stirred my imagination in a way my father's so much more approachable people quite failed to do. Even the fact that some of them were Roman Catholics appeared to me romantic: it was romantic, for instance, to know they were going to hell. It all formed a background, a picture, against which I saw my mother. She had *her* world, just as I had mine, and the world of neither, when looked at thus, was the world of our immediate surroundings.

I had a very real admiration for my mother, queer and detached as the word may sound in expression of the emotion of a young boy. But the beauty of her speech and of her manners enchanted me—she was so incomparably a more finished product of civilization than the people among whom she now lived. Her distinction was so natural, so quiet, with a sort of sweetness that permitted you to advance just so far as was desirable and no farther. I can see her still, a delicate lace cap with a mauve ribbon in it resting lightly on the brown hair that is drawn down ever so smoothly on either side of her forehead; I can see her gentle, untroubled expression; I can see her hands (she had beautiful hands and feet) folded in her lap, as she sits in the stiff Victorian drawing-room talking to some visitor. Often—having a trick of hovering round where I was least wanted—I have watched her at such a time, and to a stranger it might have seemed she had never done an hour's work in her life; that she had no large family to bring up on the smallest of incomes; no trouble nor anxiety, indeed, in the world. Yet all morning she had been helping Rebecca (our only servant, a dark, careless, easy-going woman from the South—wide-mouthed, plain, jolly, full of superstition and good-humour), and all evening very likely she would be mending and darning while one of my sisters read aloud from Dickens or Thackeray or Lever. A strange feeling would come over me then, filling me with a kind of mingled pride and compassion. I knew so much more than I was supposed to know. My whole feelings were, in truth, mixed up with an outlandish and inarticulate chivalry. It annoyed me, for example, if the visitors had driven up to the door. My mother had no carriage, and yet such things were hers by right. She had been born to them, and they had been taken from her through no fault of her own. I even felt a vague grudge against my father because of that unfortunate blockade-running. At the same time I swelled with a superb and ridiculous arrogance. Oh, I was on my mother's side, definitely—a forlorn and helpless champion. I remembered that I was supposed to have inherited the tastes and idiosyncrasies of Uncle Henry—Henry of Ashchurch—one of the mysterious relations who hovered tantalizingly in the unknown. I looked him up to discover the nature of these particular tastes, and I found him to be even farther away than I had supposed. He was my mother's uncle, my grandfather's younger brother, and had lived, shut up among his treasures, at Lathwood Hall in Shropshire. 'He was many years a grand juror of that county, but declined to act as a magistrate from his love of retirement. He formed a valuable collection of paintings, coins, and medals, all of which, together with his library, were dispersed by auction after his decease, in 1847.' So, the discreet Burke; from which I gather that Henry was more interested in the catalogues that came down from London than in the service of his fellow-men. As a spiritual ancestor associated by my mother with Uncle Henry, there was also Uncle Fred, and I looked him up too. But on the subject of Uncle Fred Clio was more reticent, mentioning merely that he was 'sometime captain, 54th regiment'.

My mother never spoke to me of her life before she was married; for that matter, I believe she rarely thought about it. She had, in all conscience, enough to think of in the present. My two eldest brothers were in business, one in the linen trade, the other in a bank, but as yet they did not earn much. My brother Charlie's school fees were paid by Uncle Forrest. Still, it was not easy to make ends meet, and we could never go away, as other people did, in the summer. My brothers spent their holidays at the Elms, Uncle Forrest's country house, just outside Derry. I spent mine at home, and by no means in the lap of luxury. It was a rare morning when I got more than porridge and bread and butter for my breakfast, and many a day I dined off potatoes and butter and milk. But I had nothing to complain of; I had now plenty of friends, though I had not yet gone to school; and other boys, big and little—particularly the rather rough and wild ones—both now and later were always pleasant to me. My mother, it is true, eyed them with disfavour. One and all, she lumped my more intimate playmates together under the category of 'street boys', and frequently she expressed the fear that I was becoming a street boy too. Still, as she could not afford to pay for my schooling, and would have died rather than send me to a National school, and as it was impossible to keep me shut up all day in the house, things were allowed to take their course. As for her estimation of my friends, I dismissed it as mere prejudice. I had plenty of prejudices myself, but they were not of a kind to prevent me from making friends with an errand boy if I happened to like him, as was quite often the case. With my mother this class-feeling was innate, half-unconscious, and inexorable. For her there were no degrees;

the possession or the absence of talents or virtues did not affect the issue in the least; you were either within the pale or you were not; and, if you were not, no careful training, no discreet burial of compromising ancestors, no manner acquired at Eton and at Oxford, could deceive her. She knew. And when she knew, her sweetness was redoubled—but she talked to you about the weather.

VI

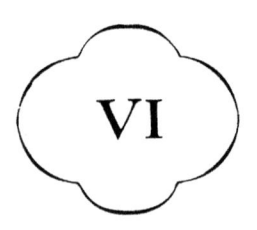

'And when one looks into the darkness there is always something there. . . .' Alas! only too well I knew it. Before Emma had gone, the darkness had presented no terror, had been merely a part of my sleepiness, through which I could call to her as she sat reading or sewing by the nursery fire. I never wanted to call, because I knew she was there; but now that there was nobody to hear me I wanted to call all the time.

Alone, in a room near the top of this not very friendly house, I seemed to be miles and miles from any human being. There were shut doors, there were many flights of stairs, to deaden effectually any sound I might make. Unless I went out on to the landing and screamed I could not possibly be heard.

The effect of this new state of things upon the darkness was immediate and startling. It was no longer a soft dim curtain hung before the gate of sleep: on the contrary, it drove all my drowsiness away. It had become like a vast rotting body swarming with obscene life. I could hear stealthy movements; I dared not open my eyes, because I knew hideous things were there, waiting, gloating, eager to display before me their half shapeless horror. From what Limbo did they flock to me, like vampires who have marked their prey from afar? These were no dreams, no creations of a child's imagination. Sleep, that used to come so easily, now seldom came till I heard footsteps on the stairs and the sound of voices, telling me the others were coming to bed—two, three hours after my own bedtime. The strain imposed upon my nervous system was appalling; the sleep which followed was rarely the sweet healthy sleep that is as much a child's right as the food he eats. Yet in the morning my fears would be shaken off; it was only when bedtime again approached that I would remember them. The dreaded hour would chime, the inevitable begging for ten minutes' grace would as inevitably be dismissed, and the grisly business of the night begin.

It began as I reluctantly pulled the dining-room door behind me (ears were quick to note whether the latch had caught or not), and found myself in a high, dimly lit hall, facing a still more dimly lit staircase. Within sight, at the end of a descending passage, was a friendly kitchen where I knew Sarah, Rebecca's successor, was sitting in laborious and audible conflict with that morning's newspaper. But the kitchen door, too, was shut; I was, so far as flesh and blood were concerned, alone.

How bright and warm and jolly everything I had just left behind me now appeared. An elder sister was reading aloud *Frank Fairleigh*, my mother was playing patience, my two eldest brothers were out, but all the rest of the family were there, listening to the story. How happy they must be, how enviable the cat blinking on the hearthrug, blinking and yawning before retiring to a dreamless couch in the bottom drawer of the kitchen dresser. If only I had been allowed to bring her upstairs with me I knew that not a ghost would have ventured near us. But I wasn't. I lingered, with every sense preternaturally alert, between the shut dining-room door and the stairs. I read the two cards: 'R.R. out'—'W.P.R. out.' Up above me yawned a deep cavernous gloom, heavy as a pall—except when broken by a white, ghastly merriment. I stood, with beating heart and bright eyes, clutching the lowest banister.

The house was a tall one—the kind of house no servant nowadays would tolerate—and nearly to the top of it I must climb. I still lingered, but ears were quick to detect lingering too, and at any rate it only made things worse. The lower flights of stairs were grey in a kind of floating twilight, for on the second landing a tiny jet of gas, turned economically down to not much more than a blue spark, shone feebly. The third flight, also, was dimly lit; but the others were black as the tomb. Besides, that miserable gas-jet burned in no amicable spirit. It was like a corpse-candle, and revealed a door open—always slightly open—which I must pass on my way up. Beyond that door was a shadowy room, in which, only too apparent, stood a wardrobe whose dark polished doors were like huge condor wings, flapping 'invisible woe'. Of that wardrobe I was terrified. How often had I seen its doors open stealthily (and oh! so slowly), while the pale waxy fingers of a dead hand just appeared between them. I hated this room even in broad daylight. Had not Sarah, going in there once at dusk, seen a long figure, with its jaws tied up and its hands folded, but its pale eyes glaring, stretched on the bed. Horrible vision, but absolutely convincing! People had died in that room, Sarah said: it smelt of death. I hurried past it with shut eyes and wildly stumbling feet: even the pitch blackness of the upper regions was better than this faint, ghastly light.

And then, what a scrambling for matches that wouldn't light—which broke, which went out. The candle would flame for a moment and sink down, as if it, too, were going out. . . .

It was all for one's good, I had been assured: I must learn to conquer this senseless, superstitious cowardice. And an easy way to conquer it was to remember God was with me in the dark. He wasn't; he never had been—unless he was a tall smiling figure with long, pointed, yellow teeth, that I saw one night standing at the foot of my bed. This, at least, was no dream. At all events, I was not asleep. If I had the requisite skill I could draw that face now, as I still half believe I could have photographed it then.

It is true I did not talk about these nocturnal terrors; on the other hand, they were much too painful for me to conceal them. Everybody knew about them, and I had not only to bear what was really a form of torture, but the reproach, as well, of being an arrant little coward. Nor was the disgraceful secret confined to my own family. I guessed this at once when I began to hear from visitors accounts of 'manly' little boys, who, so far from being afraid of it, seemed positively to prefer darkness to daylight. I detested these small heroes, and with a crimson face would vow I wasn't afraid either, which was 'naughty', being a lie.

But sometimes, after I had gone to bed, my eldest sister would sing. Up in the drawing-room, she was at all events comfortingly nearer me by two flights of stairs than anybody else, and knowing I loved music, she would leave the door open. To me it was like the opening of a door into heaven; not only because she had a beautiful voice and sang with much feeling, but because on those evenings my visitors remained away, allowing me to drop asleep in an exquisite peace. But in the winter, when the nights were longest and darkest, the empty fireless drawing-room was too cold to attract her, and, if she sang at all, she sang for only a little while.

How long this period of hauntings and nightmares lasted I cannot say (perhaps not so long as I suppose); but gradually it was left behind. I had, into the bargain, become an adept at eluding the worst kind of dreams, though at the cost, it would appear, of making sleep ever afterwards a delicate and fugitive thing, dissolving into widest wakefulness at the slightest sound. I got to know that the seemingly innocent openings of certain dreams boded no good, that *any* dream in which that wardrobe figured must be avoided. As the ogres in fairy tales can smell the blood of hidden Tom or Jack, so I could smell the silent horror approaching before it actually reached me, and was able to wake myself, and even to experience a feeble sense of triumph at having outwitted my enemies. I got, indeed, to be familiar with all the treacherous paths of this equivocal dreamland; for there were landmarks, signposts, that I remembered from past dreams, my dream-consciousness being in some sort continuous, going back from to-night to last night, to last week, to last month. And then, when I was about ten years old, I found my way into a quite different dream world, beautiful and happy enough to compensate for all that had gone before.

VII

My waking world, also, was gradually expanding, though it still remained the very small world of a provincial town—a rather hard, unromantic town too—devoted exclusively to money-making; yet a town, for all that, somehow likeable, and surrounded by as beautiful a country as one could desire. The Belfast of my childhood differed considerably from the Belfast of to-day. It was, I think, spiritually closer to that surrounding country. Then, as now, perhaps, it was not particularly well educated, it possessed no cultured and no leisured class (the sons of even the wealthiest families leaving school at fifteen or sixteen to enter their fathers' offices); but it did not, as I remember it at any rate, bear nearly so marked a resemblance to the larger English manufacturing towns.

The change I seem to see has, of course, brought it closer to its own ideal. For some not very intelligible reason, a hankering after things English—even what is believed to be an English accent—and a distrust of things Irish, have always characterized the more well-to-do citizens of Belfast. But in the days of my childhood this was not so apparent, while the whole town was more homely, more unpretentious. A breath of rusticity still sweetened its air; the few horse trams, their destinations indicated by the colour of their curtains, did little to disturb the quiet of the streets; the Malone Road was still an almost rural walk; Molly Ward's cottage, not a vulcanite factory, guarded the approach to the river; and there were no brick works, no mill chimneys, no King's Bridge to make ugly blots on the green landscape of the Lagan Valley. The town itself, as I have said, was more attractive, with plenty of open spaces, to which the names of certain districts—the Plains, the Bog Meadows—bear witness. Queen's University was not a mere mass of unrelated, shapeless buildings; the Technical Institute did not sprawl in unsightly fashion across half the grounds of my old school. Gone is the Linen Hall, that was once the very heart of the town in its hours of ease. A brand new City Hall, all marble staircases and inlaid floors, garnished with statues and portraits of Lord Mayors and town councillors, and fronted with wooden benches on which rows of our less successful citizens doze and scratch the languid hours away, flaunts its expensive dullness where that old mellow ivy-creepered building once stood, with its low, arched entrance, its line of trees that shut out the town bustle and dust. The Linen Hall Library, transported to another building, still exists, but, as with the city, expansion has robbed it of its individuality. The old Linen Hall Library, with the sparrows flying in and out of the ivy all day long, fluttering and squabbling, was a charming place. It was very like a club. Its membership was comparatively small; its tone was old-fashioned; it belonged to the era of the two- and three-volume novel; it had about it an atmosphere of quiet and leisure.

Does anybody nowadays read the romances of Jessie Fothergill, of Helen Mathers, of Mrs. Alexander? These were the books adored by my sisters, the books I saw lying about the house:—*Healey, Probation, Cherry Ripe, Her Dearest Foe, The Wooing O't*. And Rita. I have never read a line by Rita. Yet *Dame Durden* I then knew was the most beautiful novel ever written. My eldest sister mentioned this casually one day at dinner, and it never occurred to me to question the statement, so I need not question it now.

In the Linen Hall Library, curled up in a low deep window seat, I would sit gazing out between the trees and right up Donegall Place, which on summer afternoons was a fashionable promenade, where one was almost sure to meet everybody one knew. Here, hidden in a box below the counter, Mr. Gourley (then Johnnie) kept the latest novels for his favourite subscribers. Here when, at the request of my eldest sister, I asked one day for Miss Florence Warden's *House on the Marsh*, that same Mr. Gourley, knowing the library did not possess a copy, utterly abashed me by suggesting with great severity that perhaps it 'was not a nice book'. I blushed, for I was sophisticated enough to associate 'not niceness' with the improper, even while, for the sake of the family, I asserted indignantly that it *was* nice. And here, one summer afternoon, just outside the tall iron gates, I beheld my first celebrity. Not that I knew him to be celebrated, but I could see for myself his appearance was remarkable. I had been taught that it was rude to stare, but on this occasion, though I was with my mother, I could not help staring, and even feeling I was intended to do so. He was, my mother told me, a Mr. Oscar Wilde; and she added, by way of explanation I suppose, that he was aesthetic, like Bunthorne, in *Patience*.

It was years before I heard his name again, years before I came upon the short stories dedicated to Margaret, Lady Brooke; to Mrs. William H. Grenfell, of Taplow Court; to H.S.H. Alice, Princess of Monaco. At the time I saw him, he was the guest of a Mrs. Thompson of College Gardens, whose two bouncing daughters bore a distinct resemblance to my early vision of the nieces at Bootle. Flaxen haired and voluble, with their mother they got into the carriage now, while the aesthete climbed up on to the box seat beside the coachman.

VIII

I enjoyed going down town with my mother, partly because it happened so rarely that the novelty never quite wore off, and partly because now and then we wound up by calling at Linden's, the confectioner's, when Miss Boyd, who was manager there, would invariably make me a present of a box of chocolates. But my mother would sometimes refuse to go to Linden's. She knew perfectly well, in spite of my hypocrisy, why *I* wanted to go, and this little trait in my character, after all common to most children, did not strike her as attractive. There was another which struck her as still less so. I had a passionate temper, and more than once, in fights with my brother Charlie, had seized upon some handy weapon, such as a table knife, in order to equalize matters. It was after a scene of this kind, when I was still quivering with a frustrated bloodthirstiness, that I called my mother a devil. She had brought me upstairs to punish me by shutting me up in a large clothes press, built into the wall beside the lumber-room. It was then, while wriggling and struggling, though careful not to put forth more strength than she could easily cope with, that I used the word. And the very moment it had passed my lips I would have given anything to recall it. As I sat in the darkness of that rather stuffy press, surrounded by old dresses and coats and trousers, I sobbed with hatred of myself. I could easily have broken open the door, just as, before, I could easily have escaped from my mother's grasp, but so far from trying to do so, I hoped I should be left here till night. I was sure nobody else had ever spoken to his mother like that. It was not even as if the word had come out spontaneously. It had half stuck in my throat while I was forcing myself to say it. I cried till I was sick, and yet, when at the end of half an hour she came to release me, I could not tell her I was sorry, and I knew she thought I had been crying simply because of the punishment.

No such remorse, I confess, troubled me after my numerous battles with my eldest sister. Circumstances had arisen to bring me into closer touch with her, and these battles were the most immediate result. But I was not sent to school till I was past eleven, and in the interval *somebody* had to take charge of my education. The task fell to her, or rather it was thrust upon her, for she made no attempt to disguise the fact that it was in the highest degree uncongenial. I admit that I was at my worst during 'lessons'; I hated to do what I did not want to do, and invariably yielded with the illest possible grace; but, on the other hand, she was at her worst too, and never made the slightest concession to my desires. Teaching me bored her and irritated her, and the zeal with which she marked my 'noughts for conduct' usually broke the point of the pencil.

And it might be as well here to bring our whole family into some kind of perspective. Adelaide, the sister who looked after my education, was the eldest. Two years younger was my brother Bob. Then came another sister, Fanny, whose forte was to set the table—my end of it at any rate—on a roar, and who had written in a thick exercise book a singularly sentimental school story called *Longford College*. 'Good-bye, Horace darling', it commenced, and the remainder was strongly influenced by *Eric* and *Saint Winifred's*—tales which this same sister had read aloud in the winter evenings and which I had found depressing. Next, a year younger, came my brother Washington. But my elder brothers entered very little into my life in those days, and I am writing, so far as I can recapture it, only out of the consciousness that existed then. An interval of four years separated my second brother from my third sister, Connie; and a further two years brings my third brother, Charlie, who was four years older than myself, the last on the list.

There are gaps, it will be seen, and these gaps had been filled by other brothers, who had not survived, Jack, Seaton, and the famous Legend. This last was an infant who had died as soon as born, and when I first heard about him and wanted to know his name, somebody (not my mother you may be sure) had answered that his name was Legion. This in my mind became Legend, and the unfortunate Legend himself, for a space, my favourite brother. So early cut off, he appealed to imagination, and I pestered my mother with questions about him—What was he like? Why had he died? —till she lost patience and I was obliged to supply my own answers.

But the approach in time was the flimsiest of bonds: I was on far better terms with my two eldest sisters than with my youngest brother. Indeed, between Charlie and myself a sort of frozen barrier existed which I cannot now understand. For in that solid wall was not one tiniest crack or loophole. And I can see no reason for it, except that he had the type of mind which rejoices in popularity and the 'right thing', while I seldom did, and seldom said, and seldom thought the 'right thing'.

Thus between me and my sister Adelaide were some fourteen or fifteen years. She differed considerably, both in temperament and tastes, from my other sisters. She was not like them even in appearance, being dark, while all the rest of us were fair. She never came down in the mornings till at least an hour after everybody else had finished breakfast; and then her mind would be preoccupied with what she and Rita (her great friend) were going to do that afternoon. It was annoying that the first sight to meet her eyes should invariably be that of her pupil—a broad-nosed and wide-mouthed youngster, of a distinct and somewhat Socratic ugliness, who seemed bent on making the task of teaching him as disagreeable as possible, who was lazy, and at the same time sufficiently acute to point out her own defects in scholarship. Not that this troubled her. The only thing she wanted to teach me was music, and the only things I wanted to learn were natural history and Greek mythology—subjects upon which I was ready to devour the driest books, and upon which, unfortunately, I found it impossible to get any books at all. But because I had an ear, and a clear treble voice, she believed

I had a special talent for music. As a matter of fact, I had nothing but a certain sensuous rapture which I could pour out when I was alone, but which dried up on the very instant I suspected a listener. And I had no application, grudged even the futile twenty minutes I was supposed to give to my practising.

I learned little from my sister except a smattering of French. It was an odd alliance in every way—based on the queerest amalgam of sympathy and antagonism. Neither of us had the slightest patience or was prepared to make the slightest sacrifice: we understood each other fairly well—that was all. We both disliked being bored, and made no attempt to conceal it when we *were* bored; we both were *ineffably* bored by my lessons, so the result may be imagined. Once in a moment of exasperation she gave me so hard a rap on the knuckles with a ruler that I jumped up and smashed two terra-cotta plates she had brought home from a bazaar the night before. It was done in a moment of rage and pain, nor did I know she attached any particular value to these wretched plates. I knew it later, had indeed plenty of time to acquire the knowledge: she did not speak to me for a month. This was perfectly dreadful, because it was so public. Then one day she forgave me: but she forgave me in public, too. She chose an occasion when the whole family was assembled, and there were even one or two visitors present. I was so overcome by shame that on the spot I set up a howl and, with a burning face streaming with tears of mortification, hid myself from view, more furious than ever.

It was the finest stroke of all—this 'forgiveness'. Certainly I—a blunt, straightforward little male—was no match for such subtlety, was utterly routed. Next morning we treated the affair as finished, but I felt she had not let me off very easily, had made me pay not only the full price of my sin, but a pretty heavy overcharge as well.

My sister had always attracted a good deal of masculine admiration. I had begun to be conscious of this, and also, to some extent, to feel a tremulous reflection of it in my own naïve emotions. Of both these facts she was aware, and neither, I think, displeased her. She would even from time to time drop some sentimental confidence in my ear—never of a serious nature, but designed to add to my mystification. My own relation with her was as puzzling as any. She constantly, and with obvious sincerity, referred to me as an 'odious' little boy: she certainly liked me. I would sit beside the piano while she sang, and I know she liked singing to me, because she would put off other things to do so, and she was very little readier than I was myself to renounce her pleasures. She had a way, too, of consulting my taste about things, which was the more pleasing because she never asked the opinion of anybody else. And she sometimes repeated my wittier remarks, which I also found pleasing, though a shade embarrassing. Two or three times she had borne me away from my playmates on some expedition, such as a visit to one of the outlying parks. Dressed in a dark blue jersey, with a broad white linen collar turned down outside it, and blue serge shorts (rather wide in the leg, because they had been manufactured by my mother out of somebody else's old trousers), I would accompany her proudly on these occasions, when, sooner or later, our party of two would become a party of three. I would expect this, and would only wonder how long he had been waiting, for we ourselves never hurried. With what degree of seriousness she regarded these affairs I cannot tell. They were viewed, I suspect, in the light of sentimental comedy. I remember perfectly well, for instance, how, for my amusement, she named some thirty successive wooers, adding a description of each that entertained me vastly. Nor was I, now that I had reached years of discretion, myself wholly omitted from the court that was paid. From two or three of the thirty I had received gifts (always chosen with great thoughtfulness), and one of them had asked me to his rooms. I had gone. Conversation had languished, but there had been plenty of the right kind of food—by which I mean, no bread and butter to be eaten, out of politeness, first—and there had been books to bring home, books I had expressed a desire for—*Jack Sheppard*, and *The Lancashire Witches*, though of the former I made no mention, having been strictly forbidden to read it. In connection with one of these gifts, a book called *Mother Goose*, illustrated in colour by Kate Greenaway, an astonishing scene took place. My sister actually went so far as to demand it for herself—on the highly unflattering ground that if it had not been for her I never should have received *anything*. Amazement struck me dumb, but did not rob me of the power to snatch my property out of her hands. I was never more indignant. It is true she offered me in exchange a large and dilapidated volume called *Mary Howitt's Illustrated Library for the Young*, a book containing chapters on natural history, but a book which simply belonged to the house, and was no more hers than it was mine. When I had recovered a little, I wrote my name in Mary Howitt as a gift from my sister, but I kept Kate Greenaway too.

IX

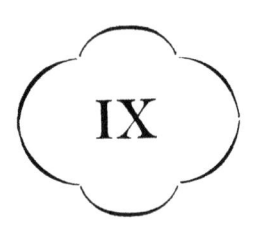

Although, when other amusements failed, I was fond enough of reading, I was not a bookish boy—not yet, at any rate. I would indeed, had it been possible, have spent my whole time out of doors. I disliked being in the house, I disliked quiet games such as draughts, I wanted excitement, and rather violent action. My real pleasures were open-air pleasures, the pleasures of the herd, of the gang, and I looked forward eagerly to the hour when my boon companions would be released from their various schools. To my mother it was a daily annoyance to hear their shrill voices uplifted from the corner of the lane that connected Mount Charles with University Street, calling my name to let me know they were there; and she was, I think, delighted when a happy chance brought under her notice a more civilized boy, one who seemed to be in every way an ideal companion for me.

To begin with, he was English, his father had been an officer in the Indian army, and was but recently dead; his mother was dead too, and he himself was at an English public school, being at present over here on a visit to his grandfather. He was older than I was, had the ordinary public-school manner, was not shy, spoke very nicely, had jumped up to open the door for my mother when she was leaving the room—in short, it seemed as if he had been sent directly from heaven. The only drawback was that I didn't care for him. But I had no reason to give, and the fact that I found his company dull only showed how far I had already fallen from a state of grace. He called at our house, and was encouraged to call again. I introduced him to my friends. Then one afternoon I received an invitation to go to look at his collection of stamps, which I accepted; and everybody was pleased.

I found him alone, and the album was produced, but I soon saw he knew nothing about stamps, and even took no interest in them. From the first his manner was preoccupied, and while I turned the gummy leaves, and made remarks on their contents, he kept looking at me, and then down at the table. Finally he got up and locked the door. I made no comment on this unusual proceeding, though I wondered what was coming, having an idea that it might be cigarettes, or even a cigar (one of his grandfather's). But he merely returned to the chair beside me, and in rather a mumbling voice began to talk. He told me that when he had been staying at his uncle's house a week or two ago, he had been wakened very early in the morning by one of his cousins, a girl older than himself, who had come to his room. He did not know how she had awakened him, but when he opened his eyes she was standing at the foot of his bed, dressed in a long, dark dressing-gown. She stood there in absolute silence, nor did he say a word as he lay staring at her. And presently she threw back her dressing-gown and he saw that underneath it she was naked. This seemed to me eccentric behaviour, though I was neither shocked, nor indeed particularly interested, and still continued to give most of my attention to the stamps. Meanwhile he pursued his narrative, a very detailed one, interwoven with a minute and quite superfluous explanation of sexual phenomena. Superfluous, because I had heard it all before, though now for some reason I felt impelled to declare that I didn't believe a word of it. This scepticism for a moment took his breath away. He produced drawings, made by one of his schoolfellows; he produced photographs. At last he got angry and called me a little fool, whereupon I called him a big one, and he threatened to chastise me. But he did not attempt to carry out his threat; he only sat gazing at me, with a strange expression of bewilderment in his dark, rather sad, rather dull eyes. I had shut the stamp book and pushed my chair back from the table. He did not know what to do. The whole thing had somehow, and quite inexplicably, gone wrong. His thick clumsy fingers, with their short nails, fumbled with the tablecloth; a profound gloom had descended upon him. At length he suggested, in the husky uneven bass of a voice that has prematurely broken, that I should take some of the stamps—any I wanted. And then I knew he was frightened.

I felt at once the keenest interest in him. I could see he was struggling against the temptation to ask me not to repeat what had taken place, and the point was for me one of supreme importance. I waited in suspense. Would he ask me or not? And all the time we sat, solemn as two owls, staring at each other. At last, with an odd feeling of relief, I saw that he had decided to trust me, and at that moment I liked him. When I reached home I was questioned as to how I had enjoyed myself, and what we had done. I replied that it had been all right, and that we had looked at stamps.

Nevertheless, I thought over some of the things I had heard, and still more over some of the things I had seen. It was not that they were new to me, but that they had been presented in an entirely new light, had passed out of the abstract into the concrete. The fact is, none of the boys who were my friends seemed much interested in such matters, even as academic questions, and if they cropped up now and again in our talk they were speedily abandoned, they remained, as it were, external and impersonal.

Our amusements, too, were as harmless as may be. It was only when there were not enough of us to make up sides in a proper game of cricket or football that they now and then took another turn. One escapade, which occurred shortly after the visit I have just described, will be sufficient to give an idea of the rest.

The backs of the Mount Charles houses, with their high jail-like walls of dull red brick pierced at regular intervals with false windows, abutted on University Street. As I see them, on the occasion in question, they are gloomy and forbidding in the dusk of an autumn afternoon that is drawing to a close. Four smallish figures are skulking in the shadow of the University Street mews, and each is in possession of a long rod—a cane without a handle. Pedestrians are few and far between; sometimes for five minutes or more the street remains deserted. But at last the four figures cross the road, and in Indian file, hugging the wall where the shadow is deepest, steal along, themselves almost as soundless as shadows. There is a pantry window beside each back-door. It is barred with heavy iron bars, and the sill is about four feet from the street level. Beneath one of these windows, which is unlatched, the little group comes to a halt. A rapid glance in every direction shows the coast to be clear; the iron bars make it easy to maintain a footing on the narrow sill; next moment one of us is on the sill, trying to peer in, though the blackness inside reveals nothing. The shelves, I explain in a hurried undertone, are on the right. Deftly a cane is inserted, and a breathless silence ensues. The cane is invisible, but we know that in the darkness it is waving industriously and noiselessly like the antenna of an insect, searching for something—something heavy, yet movable. The bars are again useful, for they offer a slight leverage, and very slowly the heavy object is teased out of position, and closer and closer to the brink. We can hear almost nothing, but we can imagine what is going on. There follows an expectant, thrilling interval of intense listening, broken by a gurgle of smothered laughter—and then an appalling shattering crash rises from the stone floor within.

I confess that this strikes me now as a shabby trick, and possibly some uneasiness of conscience, some doubt as to its legitimacy may have followed, for I do not remember that it was repeated. The baiting of Jack was more systematic. This Jack was a degraded, half-simian creature of the lowest type, with immensely long arms, and huge hands covered with thick black hair. He was dirty, evil-looking, foul-mouthed, but he had one redeeming feature—he could be excited to fury by a word or by a gesture. Needless to say these words and gestures were supplied. But Jack was dangerous, and it was well, if you intended to annoy him, to have your escape prepared beforehand, even though he could not run for more than a few yards. One day, when waiting for my companions, I was ill-advised enough to annoy him on my own account, with a result that proved to be the end of him, and very nearly the end of me.

It happened like this. Jack passed me, bearing a long ladder balanced on his shoulders, and I grabbed the end of that ladder, hanging with my weight on it so that it tilted abruptly down. Possibly the sudden jerk may have been painful; and his head being thrust between the rungs, he could do nothing, though he was powerful as a gorilla. He merely cursed me in a low voice and without so much as looking round. Therefore, having let go, I treated the incident as closed. The very slightness of the offence was the cause of my undoing, for I had forgotten all about it, and had kept no look-out for Jack's return, when ten minutes later he pounced on me from behind. He swung me round with my back to the wall, against which my head bumped dismally. I am persuaded now that this creature was not responsible for his actions; he could scarcely speak intelligibly; and the glare in his sodden eyes at that moment was certainly not sane. As I looked into his face I seemed to see what murder was like. I experienced at the same time a strange paralysing sensation, a kind of relaxation of all the muscles in my body, which prevented me from offering the slightest resistance or making the slightest sound. I could feel his grasp trembling, but it was not from weakness. He gripped my throat with one sinewy paw that almost completely encircled it, and drew my head back from the wall, selecting the spot against which he was going to dash it. It was this brief pause which saved me from being at least pretty badly hurt, for two women with market baskets appeared round the corner, and with admirable promptitude grasped the situation. What followed was not very clear to me: all I know is that the baskets were on the ground, and that both women had grabbed hold of Jack, who loosened his grip sufficiently for me to wriggle myself free. At a safe distance, though with my neck bruised and a lump on the back of my head, I turned to watch what was happening. And a surprising thing it was; for Jack seemed in the strangest way to collapse. The voices of the women were loud and shrill in abuse, but he said not a word, and slunk away with a face that had become a kind of muddy white, and without so much as a glance at me. He had been working about the houses and greens for more than a year, but he never came back.

This experience, for some reason, I kept to myself. It was natural enough that I should not mention it at home, but I mentioned it to nobody: I wanted, and was conscious that I wanted, to conceal it. Fortunately life was full and rich, filled with a kind of animal happiness which made forgetting easy. It was this animal life I shared with my mates; my other life I never attempted to share, and the two were at present absolutely divorced. Doubtless, these collective friendships of boyhood are more a matter of juxtaposition than of selection; still, in many cases, they are marked by a good deal of genuine affection. Time has not chilled in the least the feeling with which I regard these earliest friends. I liked them then; I like them now; they were as good friends, I fancy, as ever any boy had; there was only one traitor amongst them, and he again, by some strange fatality, was a boy approved of by my people, one I sometimes asked to tea. Yet he was the means of landing both George Bryce and myself in the police court. He was the informer who tried to save his own skin, and I am glad to say failed to save it. I remember Mrs. Bryce coming to our house, and bursting into tears because of the disgrace that had been brought upon our families—a little outbreak of emotion which had the excellent effect of determining my mother to regard the matter as unimportant. It was an affair of catapults and a baker, or rather the driver of a baker's van, who swore he had sustained bodily injury. We were fined, our names appeared in the papers among those of more mature offenders, and George Bryce, I suspect, received an additional and private sentence, for I saw little of him afterwards. But he had never quite been one of our group, still less had he ever come into my own private world. And just now there appears upon the scene a boy who did, who at least approached its threshold, and though he came and went swiftly, my relation with him was different in kind from the friendships I have chronicled in this chapter.

X

*O, what land is the Land of Dreams?
What are its mountains, and what are its streams?*

I do not know, but I can map out one little corner of that land, which had begun to acquire for me a strange reality.

*Look with thy soul.
For while it sleeps, the mind is lit with eyes.* . . .

So counselled the ghost of Clytemnestra, and I looked, but looked exactly as I looked with my bodily eyes when I was awake. There were two worlds, and it never occurred to me to ask myself whether one were less real than the other. It did not seem to me that either was unreal, that either was my own creation. I lived in both, and the fact that I should open my eyes night after night in precisely the same spot in dreamland was no more surprising than that I should open them morning after morning in my bedroom at home.

Of course, there were foolish dreams, dreams that travestied the ordinary things of one's waking life, and dull dreams that merely echoed them, and terrifying dreams which, as I have said, I had learned to elude. But *this* particular dreaming was pure happiness; and always the setting was the same, the time the same, the season the same; for it was always summer, always a little after noon, and always the sun was shining.

The place was a kind of garden. There were no flower-beds, there was no wall to shut it in; but there were flowering shrubs, and glades, and lawns, that looked as if they had been tended by human hands. Always when I first awakened I was in broad sunlight, on a low grassy hill that was no more than a gentle incline, sloping down to the shore. A summer sea stretched out below me, blue and calm. No white sail ever drifted across the horizon; no footsteps ever marked the unbroken crescent of the sandy beach. And inland, no trail of smoke ever rose into the coloured air. I saw no house or building, no sign of human habitation. But I did not feel lonely. I knew there were people there, and that I could find them if I went in search of them—older people, I mean, than the playmates I had so often met here in the past—men and women whom one day I should know. Meanwhile, I sat still, facing the wide blue glittering sea, and waited. I could hear a droning of bees, mingled with the splashing of the waves; I could follow the wavering, curving flight of a butterfly; I could hear birds calling softly from the woodland near.

I was waiting for someone who had never failed me—my friend in this place, who was infinitely dearer to me than any friend I had on earth. And presently, out from the leafy shadow he bounded into the sunlight. I saw him standing for a moment, his naked body the colour of pale amber against the dark background—a boy of about my own age, with eager parted lips and bright eyes. But he was more beautiful than anything else in the whole world, or in my imagination.

Afterwards the dream might wander hither and thither; we might bathe in the sea or in one of the pools, or play upon the shore, or plunge into the woodland; we might be alone, or others might join us in a game; only the beginning was always the same, or very nearly the same.

And from the moment I found myself on that hill-side I was happy. All my waking life, indeed, was blotted out. I had a sense of security, as if no doubt or trouble or fear could ever again reach me. It was as if I had come home; as if I were, after a long absence among strangers, once more among my own people. But the deepest well of happiness sprang from a sense of perfect communion with another being. It was this I looked forward to, this that I still longed for when I awoke. Having tasted it, no earthly love could ever fill its place, and the memory of it was in my waking hours like a Fata Morgana, leading me hither and thither, wherever some faint reflection of it seemed for a moment to shine.

In my dream rambles I never went far inland, remaining on the fringes of an unexplored world. The sea held me. No matter whither I might turn it was there; and even if I turned directly away from it and plunged into the woods, at the first clearing it would come again into view. And many things happened there which I could not bring back with me. I knew they had happened though I could remember so little. For to make my return journey I had to pass first through an intervening dreamless period in which nearly all was lost, and it is only from the few surviving fragments that I can piece together even this faint picture of that lovely country; as for the story behind it—the words, the actions—these are sunk for evermore in an impenetrable night.

There were animals, large and small, wild and tame, but all perfectly friendly—even the great jewelled snakes, coloured in fire, who would lift up their flat watchful heads from the long grass and gaze at me through the sunlight. These beasts were my playmates, too. I ran with them, and wrestled with them, and rolled on the grass, and in their gentle roughness they were careful not to hurt me. There were leopards and wild horses and tigers and bulls, and their strength passed into me, and their swiftness, and a power of wordless speech.

What it was like farther inland, what discoveries I might have made had I penetrated into the heart of the country, I do not know. The part familiar to me was a kind of woodland, the turf for the most part short, and with many open glades and deep clear pools. In some of these glades were stone figures watching over our playground, and guarding it from intrusion. A spirit was alive within them: they could hear me and see me, though no breath passed their lips. And there was one different from all others; one I had found in no sacred grove, but in the open, on the brow of a hill, from which it looked out steadfastly across the sea; a crouching beast in black marble, with a panther's smooth body and a human face. As it dreamed there on its pedestal it, too, was alive, had within it a flame, a spirit. It was more nearly waking than the others, for I saw the eyelids quiver. Yet when I touched the smooth flanks they were hard and cold and polished, and the curved paws were solid stone. I did not want to awaken it, for there was something terrible about it. I had a feeling that if it were to rise up and open its mouth and send forth its cry across the sea, this would be the end of all things.

When I first visited this land I have no means of telling, but my faculty for getting back there came and went curiously. There were periods, stretching over months, when I seemed to have lost it, and then for several nights in succession I would find myself on that grassy hill-side, looking down on the familiar shore. But of the beginning of it all I can tell nothing. It seems to me almost certainly to lie behind my interpretation of the tale Emma once read to me, and the feeling of recognition which that tale aroused. There must have been very early visits I had forgotten. The intervening sleep may then have been deeper. The dream itself, up to the end, remained *in* time, by which I mean that the boy in it grew older as I myself grew older. And then, somewhere about my sixteenth or seventeenth year, the whole thing was permanently cut off.

It is true that perhaps half a dozen times since then I have had a glimpse of that lost scene. But it has been like a dream of a dream. What hands in what mysterious clock in nature have on these occasions been reversed I cannot say, but I have literally gone back to those last days of the true dreaming; my thoughts, my emotions, my *understanding* even, have been precisely what they were then. As if a sponge had been drawn across some part of my mind, all the experience gathered in later years, and all memory of them, have been washed out. Moreover, the reversion has been not only mental, but physical too, for the fresh, keen, unmistakable sense of earliest youth, with its eagerness, its energy and vitality, has been renewed.

And because of this dream life my waking life only partially satisfied me. Most of its hours were vivid enough to hide away everything but their own clamour, but when I was alone I wanted something different, something that was not there, or not there in a form I could grasp. I was not even sure *what* it was I wanted, unless it were to bring my two worlds together, to recapture with my waking eyes the fugitive visions of sleep. I never could recapture them. When they seemed to draw nearest was during some brief rapturous communion with nature. I would listen, trying to hear—even if it were faint as the voice of a sea-shell—the breaking of the waves on the shores of that remote Atlantis. Then, indeed, it might be that for a few moments of mysterious ecstasy the touch of the wind or the sun would become a caress from an unseen hand, and the voice of a god whisper through the voices of earth:

I shall not fail. To the end will I protect thee.
Near shall I be, even though far away.

PART THREE

XI

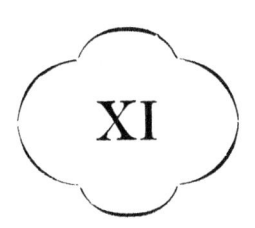

It was the middle of the summer holidays, and I felt discontented. The first weeks had been all right, but now nearly everyone had gone to the seaside. My own last visit to the sea had taken place so long ago that I hardly remembered it. Since then, for me, it had been town without a break; and I was sick of hanging about the streets through all this glorious weather, with nothing to do and nobody to play with.

The days passed slow and dismal as a funeral. They were hot, brilliant days too, with lingering, golden evenings. Yet they dropped one by one into the void—wasted, useless—while I pottered in and out of the house, ringing the doorbell a dozen times a morning, till in the end Sarah's temper became as uncertain as my own.

Things had not gone well of late. There had been the affair of the kindness of Mrs. Jenkins. My mother seemed to think I had behaved badly, though she knew nothing about Mrs. Jenkins except what I myself had told her. The Jenkins family had descended out of the blue, and the only person who took an interest in them was Professor Park, while even his interest had ceased as soon as he had secured another autograph for his collection. I had met him coming away from the Jenkins' house with the autograph in his hand, and had stopped to speak to him. At the back of my mind was a faint hope that he might ask me to accompany him wherever he was going; but he merely told me about the autograph, told me Mr. Jenkins was a novelist who had written a story called *Ginx's Baby*, which he believed to be popular, though he had not read it himself: then he passed on his way. I repeated his information at home, and my mother said *Ginx's Baby* was an odious book. After this I thought it rather unreasonable of her to be so vexed when I failed to create a good impression on the novelist's wife.

Mrs. Jenkins had invited me to go for a walk with her and her three youngest sons. The invitation was informal: she had, in fact, discovered me in the character of a pavement artist, and had stopped to look at, though not to admire, my work. Very much embarrassed, I got up from the flags, my clothes powdered with chalk and street dust. She asked me why I was making such a mess directly beneath her windows, and why, if I wanted to draw, I didn't draw in front of my own house. I explained that my own house was not on the sunny side of the street, and that I was only drawing because I had found a piece of chalk and had nothing else to do. It was then that she issued her invitation.

I don't know whether I accepted it or not—probably not —but I know that I went, because I found it impossible to refuse. I went, nevertheless, unwillingly. I was extremely shy, and conscious, with the spick-and-span examples of the Jenkins boys before me, that I was also extremely dirty. Mrs. Jenkins suggested that I might like to return to the house to brush my clothes, but I assured her this was unnecessary, and began to brush them with my hands. I could have added that there wasn't the least use in my returning to the house, since Sarah had refused to open the door for me already. So we started off, two of the Jenkins boys hanging on their mother's arms, and myself and the third boy walking one on either side of the united trio.

If I started out with reluctance, 'reluctance' quite fails to express the feeling which very soon arose within me as we proceeded in this straggling band up the Malone Road. The conversation of Mrs. Jenkins was addressed at first exclusively to me, and she spoke in a clear, authoritative voice, determinedly pleasant. Her remarks, or rather my replies to her remarks, were every now and again punctuated by a sudden staccato laugh, also determinedly pleasant, though so far as I could see there was nothing to laugh at. By this time I was convinced she had attached me to her party simply from a motive of curiosity. She asked me my name and my age; she asked me what school I went to, and was astonished when I told her I went to none; she asked me a whole series of questions, designed apparently with a view to discovering whether I had received any education at all; and as these questions became more and more elementary, it did not need the supercilious glances and veiled amusement of the Jenkins boys to tell me how badly I was acquitting myself. I dug my hands into the pockets of my trousers, partly because she had told the son who was not hanging on to her to withdraw his, and partly to show indifference.

Mrs. Jenkins, having exhausted fact, passed to the subject of fiction. What kind of stories did I like? Her boys were very fond of Henty. I could imagine they would be, and answered that I hated Henty. What books *did* I like, then? Surely I must know. Did I not read *any*thing? What was I reading at present? I answered that I was reading a story called *The Magic Valley*, and after trying vainly to drag from me an account of what it was about, she gave me up as hopeless and turned her attention to her own family.

The conversation at once became animated, intellectual, and literary. The names of Dickens and Thackeray, Tennyson and George Eliot, pattered against my ears like hailstones on a window-pane. The Jenkins boys had high-pitched voices, and they talked with the abrupt assurance, and indeed quite in the manner, of their mother. To me they addressed not a word; it was all far above my head; and if it had not been for an occasional contemptuous stare I might have supposed I was forgotten. And then the climax was reached, for Mrs. Jenkins suggested that it was time to talk French, which it seemed they always did when out for walks. I had my head down and was trying to plan some excuse for making my escape when one of the boys turned and shot a sentence in French straight at me. I dare say I knew as much as he did, but I felt the blood burning in my cheeks when I heard the others tittering while they waited for my reply. It came—in my native tongue, however, and in an undertone meant to be inaudible, but which cannot have been inaudible, for Mrs. Jenkins gave me a look that was no longer pleasant, and the boy who had spoken said, 'You know how to use bad language, anyway.'

I didn't care. I had had enough of them. For two pins I would have told the whole family to go where I had already told *him* to go. I stopped in the middle of the road, and the others, too, came to a standstill, the boys regarding me now with open scorn. Mrs. Jenkins seemed for once uncertain what to say, but her sons knew, and as if fearing she might try to detain me chimed in chorus, 'Let him go. Nobody wants him.' I didn't wait for permission; I turned my back and left them there.

But when I reached home my mother, who it appeared had watched us all start out together, wanted to know why I had returned alone. Nor was she convinced by the very halting reasons I offered; for nothing on earth would have induced me to reveal the true nature of my humiliation. She decided that Mrs. Jenkins had been kind, and that my behaviour in leaving her in the middle of our walk, without so much as thanking her, had been so ill-mannered that either I or she would have to apologize. I listened in silence, but this was not the end. For during my absence, it seemed, an old lady had called to ask that I should be forbidden to interfere with her grandson Charlie. Charlie had been told he was not to have anything more to do either with me or my associates, and his grandmother hoped that in future my mother would see that I left him alone.

Again I had nothing to say, though I assumed a feeble show of virtue. But my mother was not deceived, and that evening there was talk of school after the holidays—Miss McMullan's perhaps, or Miss Hardy's—though I was getting almost too big for a preparatory school, since at fourteen one had to leave. Nor did I want to go to school. I had been running more or less wild too long for the prospect to be anything but alarming. Of Miss Hardy's I knew nothing; of the other school only what my friend Malcolm Nelson, who had just been expelled from it, had told me. Therefore, coming out after breakfast on this radiant summer morning, I felt the whole world to be gloomy, and if it had not been for this new threat of school could have wished the holidays over.

I advanced to the edge of the green and surveyed the tedious prospect. And while I stood there, as if to make it more tedious still, a door opened on the opposite side of the street, and a chair was wheeled out and placed in the sun near a window. In this chair was a little girl all wrapped up in rugs, though how she bore the heat of them I couldn't imagine. I knew her very well, for she was often brought out like this to watch us play. She could do nothing but sit still herself; she had never been able to run about; and I had been told that what was the matter with her was some form of heart-disease. It was this, I had been told, that tinged her face to so unpleasant a hue; it was this that accounted for her whining voice, her peevish, fretful manner, her perpetual threats to 'tell'. I loathed her. Nor was my dislike merely passive. If the chair had suddenly come to pieces, if she had been run over and stamped out of existence, if a wasp had flown up and stung her, I should have been glad. Nor was I ashamed of this feeling, though I knew it was one I must conceal. I was made that way, and no more blamed myself for it than I took credit for rescuing stray cats and mangy dogs. I was made that way too, so there was an end of it.

I thought the sick child in the chair might call me (she had done it before now), so I turned my back on her. In the distance I saw Charlie about whom so much fuss had been made. Evidently he had received his instructions for he did not even glance in my direction. I mused on his discreet behaviour, and rather regretted it. He was not a bad soul in his way, but he was one of those boys who are fated to have a poor time, who, for one reason or another, are singled out by their fellows as a wood-pigeon might be singled out by hawks. In his case, so far as I can now discover, it was merely because he talked very slightly through his nose, and, being an only child and brought up by his granny, had a rather prim and proper manner. Yet because of these things his life had been made a burden to him, and he rarely returned home without traces of tears. His grandmother had made one desperate effort to establish his popularity by organizing a sort of sports and herself giving the prizes. But when the races were over, and the prizes distributed, Charlie's position became precisely what it had been before. And I could have told her it always *would* be the same. She might whisk him off on a broomstick to the Antipodes, but it would make no difference. Nor was it that anybody disliked him. I had often played with him myself, perfectly amicably, when there was nobody else, and would have been willing to do so now. It was simply that the moment a third boy appeared upon the scene the sport of baiting him became irresistible.

This morning he had brought out a bat and a ball. It was like him to do that when there was nobody to play with. I knew he was aware of my presence though he carefully avoided looking round, and I also knew that if it had not been for the instructions he had received he would by this time have been sidling up with friendly overtures. He invariably did; he was the most forgiving creature in the world. Well, there was nothing to be done here, and I moved away towards the smaller of the two greens.

From an upper window Tillie Vance waved a handkerchief at me. I pretended to be absorbed in balancing my cane and took no notice. Not long since, on a Saturday evening, a fairly large party of us—composed of both sexes—had gathered for a game of hi-spy, and at the end of the game somebody—one of the girls, I expect—had proposed that we should all go for a walk on the following afternoon. There was a novelty about the idea which made it immediately popular. We were to meet in the lane at three o'clock, and five boys had pledged themselves to be there, and five or six little girls. As a matter of fact the only person to whom the plan did not appeal was myself. I did not quite see what we were going to do when we *had* met, and it was Tillie Vance who, with a soft and subtle *câlinerie*, persuaded me.

So when three o'clock came, dressed in my Sunday clothes, and wearing a pair of brilliant new orange kid gloves, I sallied forth to keep the appointment. All the girls were there when I arrived, but not a single boy. I did not join the little group as I should certainly have done on an ordinary occasion, but held myself aloof, and at a distance of four or five yards stood waiting till one at least of the other boys should appear. I waited in vain. Very soon, indeed, I guessed that they were even now in hiding somewhere, watching out for me and my five maidens, and this thought did not help to remove my self-consciousness, though it was the behaviour of the little girls that most annoyed me. They did nothing but giggle among themselves, casting from time to time a sidelong glance at me, and particularly, I imagined, at the obnoxious gloves, which I hastily took off and stuffed into a jacket pocket. Their remarks were inaudible, but that made them worse. And prominent among the offenders was Tillie Vance. It was my first experience of the unaccountableness of woman, and I felt myself growing hotter and hotter, and I had been neither cool nor comfortable to begin with. Then, of one accord, they all turned their backs and marched off down the lane. No doubt it was partly my own fault, no doubt if I had been more of a society man I could have carried the thing off, though even then I don't quite see how I could have gone for a walk with five girls. But I might at least have joined them, and not looked such an utter fool. However, I was not a society man. At parties I was invariably one of the boys who wouldn't dance, who slunk out of the room at the first opportunity, and wrestled and played noisy games on the stairs and in the passages, who, in short, were there more or less on sufferance, and not always asked back again.

This was the reason why I now took no notice of Tillie Vance. Tillie Vance had played me false; she had professed an interest which apparently she did not feel; she had left me in the lurch at a difficult hour; and I was not to be cajoled and appeased by the fluttering of a handkerchief. So I balanced my cane, that long, slender rod I have alluded to in another chapter, and whose chief use was to throw, something after the manner of a sling, little balls of clay, which it could send an immense distance, well over the tops of the highest houses. I rolled up such a bullet now, about the size of a small plum, and fixed it in position. Then, stepping out into the middle of the road, I let fly. The shot was intended to soar far into the air, but whether my mind was still preoccupied with the perfidious Tillie, or whether I had attached the clay too loosely, I don't know. What I do know is that it sped with diabolical speed and accuracy straight for the Vances' drawing-room window, where it flattened itself out, while a beautiful starry pattern of cracked glass radiated from it across the pane. Needless to say I effaced myself as rapidly as possible, but only too well I knew that when Tillie had looked out I had been standing there, a solitary figure balancing a cane, and only too well I realized that she understood what that cane was employed for, and had even tried it herself. *Via* the ever friendly University Street I betook myself from the neighbourhood, but it was a bad beginning to the morning, and I felt depressed.

I wandered on down Botanic Avenue with no aim in view except to leave Mount Charles behind me, and as I went I remembered it was the poultry woman's day, and that she might have taken me for a drive in her cart, as she sometimes did when she was going any distance. Now, of course, I should not see her, and so another morning would be wasted. For these drives were jolly, the poultry woman was jolly, even though she always kissed me and put her arms round me and even put her hands inside my shirt to tickle me, when we came to a secluded spot. As a matter of fact, I particularly enjoyed this part of the programme, though I felt it incumbent on me to pretend I didn't. I really pretended to pretend, for I offered not the slightest resistance when, after we had turned into some shady avenue, I was pulled back sprawling across the seat, and she kissed me on the throat and other sensitive spots, while the patient old horse, standing under the trees and brushing the flies from him with his tail, waited good-naturedly, though now and then glancing round in mild surprise to see if we had nearly finished. The cooks, too, in certain of the Malone Road houses would bring me out things to eat, and occasionally take me into the kitchen. With women of this kind—plump, good-tempered, and sensual—

I was for some reason a favourite—perhaps because I liked them, and they knew I liked them.

And now I was drawn between a desire for the poultry woman and an instinct that warned me to keep away from the neighbourhood of the broken window. Then it occurred to me that I might meet the poultry woman before she reached Mount Charles, for she had customers here and there and everywhere, though principally in the larger houses. I had by this time reached the Lower Crescent, and, as usual, stopped to gaze up at Monsieur Bruneau's house at the corner. Monsieur Bruneau was a well-known and largely patronized dancing-master, and his house had fascinated me ever since I had heard that Madame Bruneau had fallen out of one of the top windows on to the pavement below. There was a story of somnambulism, and there were other, darker, and of course much more attractive stories. I used to try to pick out the particular window through which she had fallen, and I tried again now, watching her in imagination as she pulled up the lower frame, hearing the rather sickening crack and splash on the pavement, for I had been told that in falling from a height one always came down head first. Rooted to the spot, I remained wrapped in grisly speculations, directly in front of the dining-room window. The speculations were absorbing, but in the midst of them I became aware that Monsieur Bruneau, a remarkable person who had dyed his hair green, was at that window now, glaring out at me, and that Mademoiselle Bruneau was at another, tapping on the pane and making angry signs for me to go away. This was too much. I might be giggled at by stupid little girls; I might be treated with superiority by the Jenkins family; but I was not going to be tapped away by a Frenchman with green hair and his elderly daughter. I had a right to stand in the Lower Crescent as long as I wanted to, and I intended to uphold this right. My drooping spirits revived. It was exactly what I needed. For as Monsieur Bruneau appeared unable to withdraw from the window, but stood with his nose almost against the glass, I was able to indulge in a pleasing pantomime which had the effect of increasing his excitement to frenzy.

He was now, as he unconsciously mimicked all my gestures, so exactly like a monkey in a cage, that he convulsed me with laughter. Nor was it till I heard somebody opening the hall-door that I thought it better to move on, and slipped round the corner into Botanic Avenue.

This interlude had done me a world of good. I felt once more in tune with life, and began even to take a more optimistic view about the Vances' window. Tillie might not give me away. Had I not kissed her—gallantly—at Postman's Knock; had she not sent me a Christmas card; had we not gone to see a conjurer together; had we not acted together in the play of Cinderella? Nevertheless, I derived more comfort from the thought that the broken window might not be discovered till it was too late to prove my guilt. It was that wretched clay which was so damning. . . .

I slackened my pace. A train was passing under the Central Railway bridge, and I leaned over to watch it and to spit down on the roofs of the carriages. Then I perched myself on the wide low wall and kicked my heels against the stones.

I was at a loose end. Even the busy Satan seemed unable to find occupation for me. It must be now, too, very close on the poultry woman's hour if not actually past it, and I decided to return home and risk the broken window.

But there was no need to go near the Vances' house. I could go back by the University Road, and watch for the poultry woman from a spot just within the gates. Once my mind was made up I hurried, and choosing this time the Upper Crescent, in two or three minutes had again reached Mount Charles.

The first thing I saw as I turned the corner was that Charlie had picked up a companion during my absence, an unknown, fair-haired youth of freckled but pleasing countenance, whose left hand at the moment was twisted into the collar of Charlie's jacket, while with his right he administered from time to time a slow and thoughtful dab at Charlie's ribs. This not unfamiliar spectacle brought me to a pause. It was not in any sense of the word a fight (there never were fights where Charlie was concerned); it appeared almost too absent-minded to be called bullying; and I marvelled at the persistent ill-fortune which seemed to attend all poor Charlie's attempts at making friends. Over his bowed and scarlet face the intensely blue eyes of the stranger met mine in an expression of perfect good humour. But he was not on his own ground, he was a trespasser, therefore I felt it necessary to ask him what he thought he was doing.

'Nothing,' he replied, and, as if by way of illustration, administered another poke, which drew a kind of gurgling grunt from the captive.

'You'd better let him go,' I advised.

'Why?' the freckled boy asked gently. He was very little taller than myself, but he was more sturdily built and probably a year or so older, therefore his question possessed a certain pertinence.

'You're choking him,' I explained less martially, and indeed the face of Charlie had grown purple.

The other boy relaxed his hold. 'He was cheeky,' he said, while Charlie backed away. 'Not very—just a little.'

'Give me my ball,' Charlie demanded tearfully.

'You've lent me your ball,' the stranger answered. 'And now you've lent me your bat.' He made a sudden pounce, so that the bat was in his possession before the words were out of his mouth.

The swiftness with which this action was accomplished dazzled me: it was like a conjuring trick. Next moment the bat was in my own hands, but it was because he had put it there. And now, taking the ball from his pocket, he began to bowl me lobs, from which I returned catches, while Charlie leaned against the railings and watched us.

Inevitably, in spite of what had happened, in spite of the warnings I had received, the old rigmarole began.

'This bat is very like one I used to have.'

'Is it? He probably prigged it from you. He's a cunning little devil, you know: certainly he prigged this ball from me.'

Charlie began to sniff, and to edge away in the direction of his grandmother's. But I didn't want a repetition of yesterday's visit, and hastily shouted after him, 'Here!—you can have your bat.'

He returned and grabbed it from me, and the other boy, after a slight hesitation, gave him the ball too. Then he seated himself on one of the little stone pillars at the lower corner of the green and looked at both of us.

I wondered where he had come from, and there was a brief silence, which was broken by Charlie, who, jerking his head in my direction, announced, '*He* can jump nearly his own height.'

This was an exaggeration, but the stranger's simple 'I don't believe it,' was none the less vexing.

'He can,' Charlie persisted. 'Up to there anyway,' and he traced an imaginary line with his hand. Then he added, 'He's very nimble.'

'Nimble,' the other boy repeated under his breath, while I hastily told Charlie not to be a fool.

But that was his way: he always used such words—words that sounded queer and pedantic—nothing could get him out of the habit.

'What's the nimble person's name?' the strange boy presently enquired, addressing nobody in particular.

I felt myself flushing. I didn't like this tone at all. But Charlie, with unnecessary eagerness, mentioned not only my name, but also where I lived, pointing to the house.

The stranger did not trouble to turn his head.

'What's *your* name?' I asked him uncomfortably.

He waited for a minute or two, during which he regarded me with an expression of placid detachment. I was sure he was going to tell me to mind my own business; but he didn't; he rose from his seat; 'Alan Cunningham,' he said. 'We'd better go and get some lemonade; there's a place just across the street.'

He turned at the same time to Charlie, as if to show that he too was included in the invitation, but Charlie, casting a reproachful glance at me, shook his head. 'I can't,' he said in a mournful voice.

'Why? It won't do you any harm. You can have something else if you don't like lemonade.'

'I'm not allowed to go with *him*.'

This caused the unknown boy in his turn to look at me, and with, I imagined, a faintly increased interest. 'That's a pity,' he replied.

We made no further attempt to induce the obviously wavering Charlie to alter his decision. We left him there, gazing after us wistfully, as we went out through the gates and crossed the road to the confectioner's.

It was a good-sized shop, but at present there was only one person in attendance, Mr. Brown, the proprietor. My new friend, concerning whom I could not quite make up my mind, ordered the lemonade, and we watched it being poured out into two brimming glasses. I had just taken my first sip when Alan leaned forward, and pointing to a shelf directly behind Mr. Brown's head asked, 'What are those?'

Mr. Brown turned mechanically, and at the same instant Alan lifted a large flat package of chocolate from the counter and slipped it beneath his jacket.

'Which do you mean?' asked Mr. Brown vaguely.

'Those green sweets. But it doesn't matter; I don't want any.'

There was not a glimmer of expression in his face or in his voice as he spoke. He continued to drink his lemonade slowly, and to make an occasional remark to Mr. Brown, asking him about the confectionery business. As for me, standing by the counter, my tumbler in my hand, I was too astonished to raise the glass to my lips till a quiet voice saying 'Don't you like it?' made me gulp down a mouthful. Of course I coughed and choked, and then for the first time Alan's eyes rested on mine, and for a moment the lid of one of them flickered. But I could never tell, either then or later, what thoughts were passing in his mind. My own face, I dare say, was more expressive, and it was probably just as well that the lemonade had gone down the wrong way. For I was profoundly shocked, and what helped to trouble me was the fact that this boy had done what he had done so openly, without knowing whether I should object to it or not, without really knowing anything about me, and apparently without caring either. He knew I could not give him away, and that was all that mattered. But supposing Charlie had been with us? What then? I had an uneasy feeling that then it wouldn't have happened. Only, why . . .?

We finished our lemonade (in my case with no great enjoyment) and came out into the sunlit street. It was my dinner-time, and I said so.

'I'd better be getting back too,' he answered; but he continued to walk beside me. Not a word about what had taken place passed between us, though the embarrassment and constraint appeared to be wholly mine.

'Shall I come round this afternoon?' he asked. 'Will you be here if I do?'

I hesitated, but he did not seem to be conscious that my reply was rather long in coming. He even put his hand on my shoulder as we walked slowly on up Mount Charles. Then I said 'Yes', but I did not look at him as I said it.

It was just before we reached the house that he took the package of chocolate from inside his jacket, and breaking it in half, handed one half to me. I shook my head and rang the bell.

'I'll chuck it away if you don't.'

'You can do as you like,' I answered. 'I don't want it.'

He stood for a moment in silence. 'Well, I'll leave it here on the window-sill. Somebody will see it and take it.'

Just then my eldest sister opened the door. He smiled at her and lifted his straw hat, and without the least hesitation offered her the chocolate. The action was somehow simple, natural, charming. 'Forrest won't take it,' he explained, speaking my name for the first time.

I entered the house, feeling unusually thoughtful.

XII

A sudden noise must have awakened me, for it was hardly daylight, and, though I was in my own bed, the vision of the scene I had just left still floated before me, and there was something about that vision which I could not understand.

There had been a deep blue pool, and I had been bending over the margin of it, perhaps to drink, perhaps merely to see if anything lived there; but when I had leaned down I had looked straight into the eyes of a dark and almost swarthy face, which, as I remembered it now, bore no resemblance to my own. And yet it had caused me *then* no surprise, it had been the image I had expected to see. And with that I remembered the whole body, the brown bare limbs stained with earth, the widespread toes, and hopping out of bed I ran across to the dressing-table. My brother, with whom I now shared an attic, was still fast asleep in the other bed, his head, as usual, buried beneath the clothes. I took off my nightshirt and tilted the looking-glass under the skylight so as to be able to see as much of myself as possible. Of course, I didn't really expect a miracle to have happened; I don't quite know what I expected; but suddenly a voice behind me broke in on my silent pantomime: 'What on earth are you doing?'

I wheeled round. My brother Charlie was sitting up watching me; and, a little discomfited, I scuttled back under the blankets, and lay turning the problem of my dream over in my mind.

Was I always like that when I was there? I could remember nothing from any other dream that threw a light on the question, but I somehow felt that this dream, too, would have told me nothing had I not been wakened in the middle of it, and wakened by chance at the precise moment when my own image was before my eyes. There was no evidence either for such a theory or against it. All I could decide was that I very much preferred this dream shape, and would change my own for it even now, and at the risk of not being able to establish my identity. I lay half inventing, half dreaming the scenes in the strange story that would follow—a story which grew more and more detailed and 'actual', with a hint of tragedy in it at last—until I felt somebody jerking the bedclothes and heard Charlie's voice telling me it was time to get up.

Now and then, while we were dressing, I looked at him, but he said nothing of the antics he had witnessed at dawn; he may have forgotten, or even fancied he had dreamed them; at any rate, my behaviour at all times appeared to strike him as so inexplicable that this particular example of it he probably accepted with the rest. I knew he regarded me with a dubious eye. Our bedroom, in fact, was not unlike a cage at the Zoo in which two animals of different species have been placed and maintain a sort of restless, difficult peace by carefully avoiding each other. He was now an apprentice to the linen business, but would have liked to be in the Army or the Colonial Mounted Police. His tastes were for field sports—hunting, horse-racing, etc.—and though he had no chance of gratifying them, he had bought a gun so as to be able to get a day's shooting when an opportunity presented itself. Me he ignored as far as possible, and, though we shared the same room, we scarcely ever exchanged a word.

As usual the stir and bustle of a new day threw a veil over the secret glamour of the night, and I came down to breakfast thinking only of what Alan and I would do that morning, for it was raining, and the plan we had concocted of taking out a boat and bathing in the river would have to be revised. I saw a great deal of Alan now: in fact I saw him all day long and every day. Once he had decided to bestow his friendship on me I followed where he led, and it was a friendship that appeared to cut me off from everybody else. The things we did were somehow not of a nature to be shared with others. He did not care for games, except the games he invented himself—if one could call them games, for they were more after the manner of exploits or adventures, in which I found myself invariably playing a secondary part. What it amounted to was that he cared only to do things which involved a certain amount of risk; and sometimes, so far as I could make out, there was no other attraction than this risk. I have seen him, for instance, getting out of a second-storey window and walking along a narrow stone ledge that to me, quaking down below, appeared to be no more than four or five inches wide. Feats of this kind I found it quite impossible to emulate, and this particular one made me sick even to watch it. I suppose it was a form of the gambling spirit, and I certainly admired though I could never quite comprehend it, especially as the person who appeared to get most of the thrills was myself. If there was a cricket match or any kind of open-air entertainment, he would attend it simply for the pleasure of effecting an entrance without payment; if there was a spot where to be caught trespassing meant a chase, that spot would infallibly be marked down for a visit. And these things were done methodically, as a matter of course; never, it seemed to me, on the impulse of the moment. Other boys had plenty of pluck, but it was different; it betrayed, as a rule, a heat, an excitement, one could at least imagine it at times failing them, it was somehow (though I did not think so then) at once finer and less perfect than this cold imperturbable self-reliance of Alan's.

Curiously enough, he was very fond of reading. Though he was only a year and a half older than I was, he had read, I should think, twice as much. And he was extremely reserved in his talk, never spoke about himself, about his life at school, about his life at home, about anything but what lay immediately before us, though I tried again and again to get him to do so. For his very aloofness had a strange effect upon me; I imagined it to conceal all the qualities I most desired to find. Half unconsciously I pursued this process of idealization, until at last I came even to think he must in some mysterious way be connected with my dream-world, and the longing to put this fantastic notion to the test began to haunt me.

Such thoughts would come to me not so much during the day as during the long summer evenings, when we would sit side by side, under a creepered garden wall, with a book between us. These hours—so different from the strenuous, crowded hours that preceded them—had for me a kind of hushed enchantment which I fancied my companion must feel also. I did not really read, but only watched him reading. All the beauty of the earth seemed to flow in upon me—an almost intolerable beauty, that pressed close and closer upon my mind and senses, with its sadness and rapture. And my companion was a part of this beauty, a part of the summer, a part of the trailing evening glory, a part of the sleepy cawing of the rooks, a part of the drifting incense that rose and spread from the many-coloured flower beds. Then, through the stillness, I would hear, as if from an immense distance, that low faint backwash on my golden shore, and would be almost certain that my two worlds had begun, ever so little, to overlap. A curious idea came to me, that if I should speak certain words, taking it for granted that Alan would understand them, straightway he *would* understand them. It was the old doctrine of the efficacy of faith, but I could never quite summon up courage to say aloud what was hovering on the tip of my tongue. Once I got as far as, 'Why is it never———' and then stopped. I was going to ask, 'Why is it never night there?' I was going to ask what it was like at other times, at the times one *wasn't* there. But an instinct, or a shyness, kept me silent; and even that beginning of a communication left me vaguely troubled, as though it had broken a secret spell. Yet, after all, if it were a real place, why should not my dream-world be visited by others; why should it be mine only? For the first time I felt that I wanted to draw a being from the waking world across its threshold, and this being was the boy beside me. I watched him as he sat there, his fair head bent over the pages of his book, too absorbed in what he was reading to hear, or at any rate to notice, the faltering and hardly audible words I had spoken. I did not repeat them; I knew I never should repeat them. A premonition of unhappiness seemed to touch me; it was as if a breath of winter wind had found an entrance to our sheltered garden, sighing for a moment over our heads. And suddenly, and I think for the first time, I was aware of loneliness. I do not mean to say that it was a poignant, or even very definite feeling: it was not in the least like that spiritual anguish which had sometimes darkened my mind when I had found myself thrust back again upon the waking world. I was not precociously introspective; beyond my likes and dislikes I was not, I think, at this time even conscious of myself—conscious of myself, I mean, as somebody possessing personality, character, a capacity for good and evil: indeed I had never thought about it. But this was my first close friendship, and it had failed, I knew now that it had failed, that it had never been, even in an hour such as this, more than an echo, the shadow of a dream. And it would end when the summer ended. It would end when Alan went back to school, to his own home, which was not even in this country. Already we were in the last days of August; already one or two of my old playmates had returned from the shore.

I had held aloof from them, absorbed in this friendship with Alan. We wandered far afield. We had hiding-places of which we each possessed a plan—hiding-places where we kept things (usually of his supplying), a hollow tree, a trap-door in the floor of a deserted windowless house. Under the trap-door were hidden complete disguises—two old suits of clothes, false beards and moustaches, masks, a pistol, and a knife. We would assume these, and for me they were quite sufficient, but not for Alan, who tired of them almost immediately after we had got them, and began to throw out hints about trying something less childish, and ended by revealing his true plan. The disguises, it seemed, had never formed a part of it; the disguises had been a concession; and indeed I now remembered they had been my own idea. What he wished to do was to try an experiment in house-breaking, and, if it succeeded, to follow it up with another. I listened, but though he seemed quite serious, I could not take him very seriously—not even when he mentioned the house with which he proposed to make a start. The people, he said, had been away since the beginning of the month; there was a gardener who pottered about during the day, but he left between five and six, which gave us the whole evening; and there was, above all, at the back, an unlatched window.

So he put it, with his arm round my shoulder, where he always placed it when he wanted to persuade me to do anything; and I made no objection to joining in this enterprise. It never occurred to me that it would get beyond the stage of reconnoitring, and even up to the moment when I crept after Alan through a hole in the hedge no other thought entered my mind.

We slunk behind the bushes to the rear of the house, where a yard wall rose before us, and it was only when I saw Alan preparing to climb this wall that the adventure, for me, began to take on a less pleasing aspect. For one thing, though we both wore canvas shoes with rubber soles, I found the wall difficult. I couldn't reach within several feet of the top of it, and it was not till Alan hung over and gripped my hands that I was successful. Once inside the yard, too, there seemed to be nothing left but to get out again. Alan pointed to an upper window (probably the window of a bathroom) which was slightly open at the top; but, as we possessed neither wings nor a ladder, I could not see what difference it made whether it were open or shut. Alan, however, by means of a rain-pipe, which ran down from the roof between the window and the angle formed by two walls, had already begun the ascent. I watched him. It was unpleasant watching him—worse than doing it myself, though of course I never could have done it. His progress was painfully slow, and I could see his feet feeling for some roughness in the bricks and not always finding one. I stood immediately below him, for, if he fell, I imagined I might to some extent break his fall. And he persisted, gaining a few inches at a time. It seemed to me that he had been climbing for a quarter of an hour before he reached the level of the window, yet he did not stop here, but climbed higher still; and it was now that the worst moment was reached. Hitherto the angle formed by the two walls had helped him, but here he had to stretch one foot out sideways, groping for the window-sill, and then, holding on with only his left hand, to reach out his right hand till it could grip the sash. It looked to me as if he were stuck there, able to move neither backward nor forward, and I knew it was impossible for me to help him unless I could find a ladder. But suddenly I saw him let go the pipe, and next instant he was on the window-sill, and looking down at me with a broad smile on his face.

I smiled also, for I was glad that this at least was over, and in another minute I heard the sound of the key turning in the lock of the back-door, and then of the bolt being drawn. Alan came out, obviously very pleased with himself, though all he said was, 'We'd better unlock the yard door too, just in case we may need it.'

He did this, and then returned to me, plucking me by the sleeve to follow him. There was plenty of daylight still, if not so much as there had been, yet I stepped inside that house without enthusiasm. The kitchen was all right, because the windows were unblinded; the twilit hall was not nearly so right, and I began to hope Alan would not want to stay long. This was not very brave, I dare say, for now we *were* in, the only real danger seemed to be past; and yet, to find yourself in a strange house which you have entered by stealth, even though you know it to be empty, is not conducive to a feeling of security, and for me, though I could not have said why, there was something about this house in particular which failed to inspire confidence.

I watched Alan softly trying the latch of the hall-door. 'It's locked from the outside,' he said. 'We can't get out that way, and we daren't undo the shutters in the dining-room. However, nobody's likely to come.'

This was a strange suggestion to make at the eleventh hour, and after assuring me there would be no danger; nevertheless, it was not the thought of a surprise visit that might be paid us by one of the members of the family, or by the gardener, or by a prying policeman, that weighed upon my spirit: it was something in the house itself, something that seemed to be already there, that, in fact, had never left it.

A very horrible idea had imposed itself upon my mind, and this idea was simply that we should find a body here. I had not thought of it a moment ago, but once I *had* thought of it, the thought remained. *The Tell-Tale Heart, The Black Cat, The Murders in the Rue Morgue*—only yesterday I had read these and several other charming pieces selected for me by Alan. I wished, as I peeped into the darkness of the shuttered and blinded dining-room, that I had not read them, or at least that I had not remembered them just here and now.

Meanwhile, with the help of a lighted candle-end, he had been rummaging in the sideboard cupboards, and at present was seated happily on the carpet munching the contents of a biscuit-box which had been forgotten. I watched him, but felt no desire to join in the feast. He slid his eyes round at me as I hovered just within the doorway, and smiled slightly, though he said nothing. None the less I knew he knew I was nervous, and I vowed not to show it openly, for there was something in his face suggesting that he rather expected I should. When he had finished the last biscuit (there were not many and they must have been very stale), he rose to his feet and brushed the crumbs from his jacket. Then he blew out his candle. 'We'll go upstairs,' he said. 'There's nothing here.'

I didn't want to go upstairs: I never wanted anything less. I wanted it so little that in spite of my vow I could not help muttering, 'What's the use? We may as well clear out.'

'Clear out!' Alan repeated in astonishment. 'What for? It'll be safer, anyway, to wait till it gets dark.'

I made no further protest, particularly as he had already begun to climb the stairs. He did not stop at the first landing, nor at the second, but on the third he softly turned the handle of a door, and, as I craned over his shoulder, on the instant all my imagined horrors came true, for there, sticking out from under a bed, was a human foot.

I suppose I must have gripped Alan's arm, or pointed, or made some kind of noise, for he looked round at me in mockery. Then he stepped across the floor, and raising the pleated valance, revealed a pair of boots in lasts, one of which had fallen sideways.

I was bitterly ashamed. From the beginning this adventure had proved to be not in my line, and now I knew I had given myself away hopelessly. But just on this account perhaps, just because of this feeling of shame, my mind seemed suddenly to be cleared of its morbid imaginings, and the house to become an ordinary empty house. I stepped out on to the dim lobby, and leaning over the well of the staircase gazed down into the dimmer shadows below. I do not know why, but another spell, too, seemed to have been broken, and as I waited here till Alan should have finished, a sense of unhappiness and disillusionment swept over me, shutting out everything else. Even had I seen a ghost ascending the stairs, or heard the sound of someone at the hall-door, I do not think I should have cared. What I knew as I hung there over the banisters in the soft grey darkness, was that I was far enough now from my dream place, and that that figure I had left in the room behind me, moving swiftly and stealthily hither and thither, searching and prying, ransacking drawers and cupboards, was far enough removed from my dream playmate.

Presently I came back to the open door, and as I did so I saw him slipping something into his pocket. I watched him without surprise. It was, indeed, as if I had come back expecting to see just this, for even out there on the landing I had known that everything was at an end. All I felt now was an obscure unhappiness—a sense of loss, though I did not know what I had lost, for surely I could never really have confused my dream-boy with this other boy, who seemed hardly more than a stranger to me, whose very company I no longer desired.

But I entered the room. 'You can't do that,' I said quietly.

'Do what?' he answered, paying little attention to my words.

'You can't take anything.'

He turned round and looked at me. 'Why?' he asked.

'Because—these things don't belong to you.'

He paused. 'All right,' he said at last. 'Don't worry: I'll put it back.'

'On your honour, you won't take anything?'

'On my honour. . . . But it's rather a waste, isn't it?'

'You don't mean to say you *intended* to take anything?' I asked, with a sudden suspicion of the truth. 'I mean, it wasn't for that you wanted to get in?'

'I know it's quite different from robbing a fruit garden,' he said, with a faint sneer.

'It *is* different,' I answered. 'And it's rotten—rotten even to poke about among other people's things the way you've been doing.'

He remained silent for a moment or two, while an unpleasant expression came into his face. 'I'd forgotten you were such a saint—when it comes to doing things you don't want to do.'

'Shall we go?' I suggested.

He hesitated again. His face had already cleared. He put his hands on my shoulders and looked at me squarely. 'You're queer, you know,' he said good-humouredly, as if I were years younger than himself. 'There's a soft streak in you somewhere. I can't quite make out what it is, but I've noticed it before.'

'You didn't tell me.'

'No, but I've noticed it. . . . Just now when you came into the room, too, you looked as if you were going to cry.'

I had begun to feel profoundly miserable. 'It wasn't, anyway, about what you think,' I muttered. 'It was something else.'

'What?'

'I don't know.'

And really I didn't know. At all events I could not tell him. We descended the staircase and let ourselves out at the back. The adventure was over.

But as I walked beside him everything was altered. It was as if I had emerged from some spell-bound wood into a disenchanted land in which I saw things exactly as they were. And it was in this cold and rather dreary light that I saw the boy beside me, nor could I even understand what I had before found so attractive about him. Yet only two evenings ago I had been on the point of pouring all my confidences into his ear! For this escape at least I was thankful. And I wondered, as we walked home together, if he had really put everything back as he had promised to do. I did not think he had, but perhaps I was wrong. Our remarks became more and more perfunctory, and when we reached his gate we paused and faced each other across the wooden bars, for he had not asked me to come in.

'What's the matter with you?' he said abruptly.

I pretended to be surprised. 'With me? Nothing.'

There was a silence, and I fancy he knew, as I certainly knew, that we should not see each other again. We said good-night, and I turned on down the road towards my own home.

The twilight was gone. A thin silver moon had risen above the motionless trees, and though I was already late I sat down on a bank under a garden hedge, through which came a penetrating sweetness—the scent of mignonette.

PART FOUR

XIII

Miss Hardy's was a mixed school, but of the eighty or ninety scholars who attended it not more than a score were girls. I became one of these scholars, and because I happened to conceive an admiration for Miss Jessie Hardy, the elder of the two principals, straightway developed an exemplary studiousness. Unfortunately, there were already one or two shining lights with whom I was obliged to compete, handicapped by neither the right kind of temperament nor the right kind of preliminary training. In particular, there was a child named Mabel Johnson, who was never known to lose a mark. This prodigy had a squeaky voice and a dying-duck manner, but she had a memory like a mouse-trap, and to attempt to surpass her on her own ground was hopeless. I was astonished, therefore, when one day, by the faintest intonation in her voice, while she was correcting a French exercise of Mabel's, I discovered that Miss Jessie, though she praised the exercise, did not like Mabel. So, intellectual distinction was not the tremendous asset I had believed; and presently I was able to assure myself that if there was to be a favourite at all, it would not be any of the little girls, but a boy. Further and further eliminations followed, till the field at last seemed clear. And of all this not the faintest whisper rose to the surface: nobody knew anything about it—least of all, I imagine, Miss Jessie herself.

Nevertheless, the absence of rivals did not seem to help me very much. I was regarded as a promising pupil, and that was all. To me it meant nothing. A relation of affection was essential to me with anybody I cared for, and if I could not bring this about, no matter what kindness I received, I felt disappointed and discouraged. I had long ceased to hanker after Emma, but subconsciously her influence was still there in this unsatisfied and inarticulate desire which haunted all my boyhood. Superficially, my life had become more ordered and harmonious, but in reality, that is to say spiritually, there was no harmony; my deepest desires and instincts found nothing to feed on but themselves.

Was it now, or a little later, that I had my only serious illness, which came upon me with the suddenness of a thief in the night? I had gone to bed in the evening feeling much as usual: in the morning I had awakened with a pain low down in my right side. The pain was dull when I lay still, but it became acute if I made the slightest movement, and it was somehow sickening in a way a more external pain cannot be. I could not walk, and was carried down to the large front bedroom below my own, while a message was sent to Uncle Seaton (who lived not far away, in the end house of Queen's Elms), asking him to come round to see me.

I have written 'Uncle Seaton', but in those days I should not have recognized him by any other name than Uncle Doctor. He was an old man—fourteen years older than my father—but still hale and hearty, with a thick mop of beautiful silky white hair, dark twinkling eyes, a complexion that suggested after-dinner port, and an extraordinarily pompous gait and manner. He was abrupt, self-willed, and had never been known to furnish a patient with an account. If they paid him, well and good; if they didn't, it was doubtless because they found it hard to do so. This point of view was not shared by his wife. Aunt Lizzie wore a wig, had small bright black eyes, rosy cheeks, features that were somewhat nut-crackerish, and she reminded me, I don't quite know why, of Judy. It was partly her voice, I dare say, for she was in reality distinctly good-looking. Wherever she went she was accompanied by a diminutive black-and-tan terrier called Jip— very old, very cross, and a product, I believe, of art, like those grotesque dwarfs who were shaped in mediaeval times for the amusement of princes. Jip had none of the usual canine virtues; he was peevish, spiteful, ungrateful; nevertheless, Aunt Lizzie lavished upon him an affection she by no means extended to nephews and nieces.

Nor was much love lost, I fancy, between my mother and her. I was present on one occasion when there promised to be a definite quarrel between them. It arose in this way. There was to be a dance at Queen's Elms, and my eldest sister, having incurred Aunt Lizzie's displeasure, had not been invited to it. An invitation had arrived for my second sister and my eldest brother, but this had been refused; apparently with a little note from my mother to explain why. I was at the dining-room window when the carriage drove up and Aunt Lizzie hurriedly descended from it. I was still hovering there, half hidden behind the heavy crimson curtains, when my mother got up to receive her. The contrast between them was marked. My mother was, as usual, very quiet; Aunt Lizzie was not. 'Well, Fanny!' she burst out in a high metallic voice. . . . But I was bundled from the room before I had time to hear the rest.

I have always regretted it. There was much that I missed in those days, although I missed a good deal less than was either supposed or intended. But there was no use asking questions, and my observation was necessarily limited to fragmentary if thrilling glimpses, which are difficult now to weave into a logical pattern. It is as if one were to find fluttering in the wind a few scattered leaves torn at random from some old sentimental comedy. One such leaf is my memory of J. B. Lyons hiding under the dining-room table when his future mother-in-law, who suspected and disapproved of his visits to our house, paid us, herself, a surprise visit. Another is of this same J. B. Lyons holding my eldest sister prisoner in the drawing-room, while an hilarious band, including Tom Ritchie (always, because of his high spirits, my own favourite), gathered outside on the landing and tried to force an entrance. Such scenes were gay and exciting and I enjoyed them hugely; yet beneath them there was something serious—a something which, in fact, later took a tragic turn, and which I could not fathom. I saw the so animated surface, but at what was going on beneath it, at the intrigue, the plot, I could only make the wildest guesses.

Even as it is, I am afraid, it has led me into a too lengthy digression, from which, if I am to take things in their order, I must return to the room whither I had been carried on this first morning of my illness, and which looked very large and bare in the white bleak light flowing through the tall north windows. In that light Uncle Seaton bent his silvery mane down over me while I told him where the pain was, though my telling was not sufficient, and I can still feel the firm cold contact of his fingers against my flesh, the gentle yet sickening pressure on my body as he moved them from spot to spot, while he repeated each time the question, 'Does that hurt?'

My mother, standing behind him at some distance, motionless and half invisible, suggested that I had perhaps strained myself when moving a heavy chest of drawers on the previous afternoon; but Uncle Seaton shook his head; what I was suffering from was an inflammation of the bowels. And for weeks I lay on my back; in the beginning, while I drowsed and dozed, the passage of time being hardly noticeable, so like was one hour, one day, to another. I slept and waked and slept again, and the red flicker of the fire on the ceiling moved through my waking and dreaming thoughts, which at first were barely distinguishable. Then gradually I began to emerge from this shadowy world, my body still quiescent, but my mind alert. And one memory stands out from all others—I do not know why, for it is of a very little thing. But I remember my mother stooping over my pillow, her cool hand laid on my head, her soft voice saying 'Poor old man.'

They are not very striking words, doubtless, yet they moved me as few words have ever moved me in my life. I waited till I was alone and then I cried a little. And I thought of them for hours. Somehow, they carried me back to the days of Emma. Nobody had spoken to me quite like that since Emma's days, and nobody, as a matter of fact, ever spoke to me quite like that again.

But I was still very weak, and had more excuse then than now for relapsing into sentimentality. I *was* sentimental, you see: it was probably the mysterious streak Alan had discovered, and which had annoyed him so much. The prolonged immobility had weakened me even more than the prolonged abstinence from solid food; but the period of convalescence is always pleasant, I was well supplied with books, and, if I had not been much of a reader before, I now read omnivorously.

I began with *Paradise Lost*, borrowed for me from Professor Park. But *Paradise Lost*, too, harks back to Emma; for it was she who had told me about it, her description that led me now to ask for it. As it turned out that description was misleading. It had led me to expect a supernatural tale filled with wonder, terror, and breathless excitement. The very first words of the 'Argument' were a damper, and though I persevered, I did not find *Paradise Lost* exciting. I am sorry to say I did not even find it poetical. Compared with *Ulalume* or *The Sleeper* or *The Raven* or even *The Bells*, it was dull; and presently compared with *anything* it was dull—even with *Robinson Crusoe*, even with the stories of Henty. Of much of it I could make neither head nor tail, and what I did understand failed to interest me, so that I had the greatest difficulty in finishing the first book. I read it at the wrong time and at the wrong age, with the consequence that for some years, until I came by accident on the *Morning of Christ's Nativity*, I did not open Milton again.

My next experiment, this time with the romances of Victor Hugo, was more successful. My mother was rather doubtful of their propriety, but promised to look through them to see if there was anything I ought not to read. Some light may be thrown on my own conception of adult notions of propriety when I say that on hearing this I at once abandoned hope. For I had myself chanced on a reference to a child being suckled by its mother, and was convinced that in grown-up eyes such a reference would be considered improper. My mother, however, after turning over the pages of *Ninety-Three*, seemed to be reassured. She decided in favour of Victor Hugo.

I read all the novels: in a sense they were the first books I ever did read, for now, for the first time, I became conscious, through the work, of the mind behind it, of a something that was not the story, though the story was necessary to reveal it. My favourite was *Toilers of the Sea*. I saw no melodrama in it; I was aware only of its beauty and passion and sublimity. From this on, no novel that had not a tragic ending satisfied me. I read Helen Mathers' *Comin' Through the Rye*; I read all the novels of Miss Broughton from *Not Wisely but too Well* to *Second Thoughts*. I did not think Miss Broughton so good as Victor Hugo, but she believed in a tragic climax, and she was even more passionate. For this reason I was disappointed in *Red as a Rose is She*. The book had ended nobly with the tardy lover 'clasping a lifeless woman to his breast', but on turning the page I had found a wretched postscript beginning with the words, 'There are two sorts of lifelessness'. It was as if by not really dying Esther Craven had done me a personal injury.

One afternoon when I was deep in *Doctor Cupid* Mr. Farrington, the curate, called to see me. He was a short, thickset, but rather sickly-looking young man, with black hair and a white face. He was fervently religious, but in spite of his fervour, or possibly on account of it, my mother did not like him. For he was low church, evangelical, uncouth; and when he preached his sermons, which were delivered extempore and with an unrestrained emotionalism, his white face would seem to grow whiter, a perspiration would break out on his forehead, and he would use very plain words, such as 'fornication', which were felt to be in the worst possible taste. I did not like them myself, principally because I thought it incumbent upon me to try to look as if I didn't understand them; but other people liked them still less, and a hint was dropped to the rector.

Mr. Farrington's religion was, in fact, a great deal too mediaeval even for the most religious amongst us. It was a passion which I fancy warred with other passions. I could imagine him receiving the stigmata, or being tempted by fiends; certainly he seemed singularly out of place in a drawing-room, for he had no small talk, had received very little social training, and was, in season and out of season, terribly in earnest, as if haunted by a vision of damnation. His religion was a burning thing—a thirst, a desire, a rapture, and I dare say subject to appalling relapses and miasmas of despair. Still, I fancy one might have confessed a crime to him and not been received with the platitudes of outraged respectability. That was just the point. I remember him one evening (it was on the first and the last occasion he was ever asked to our house) bursting out in passionate denunciation of the Satan worshippers of Paris. Not a soul present except himself had so much as heard of this mysterious sect; not a soul had ever heard of the Black Mass or of the rites that accompany its celebration. As his words poured forth in a low husky voice, and with a strangely sibilant effect, a kind of frozen silence descended upon the room. More bad taste, I divined, and the questions hovering on the tip of my tongue languished. Not that the new religion really attracted me; on the contrary, it seemed even more ugly and joyless than the old, and was apparently dominated by much the same idea of sin—an idea that to me had always proved a stumbling-block, because I had never been able to feel sinful. As for believing that a person like Emma was sinful, that seemed to me sheer nonsense. In what way was she sinful? She was sinful, it appeared, for no better reason than that we all were sinful, from Adam on—all except Christ. And that was a second stumbling-block, for in spite of his sinlessness I did not feel drawn to Christ. I could not banish from my mind the pictures of him I had seen—with always something over-sweet about them, something mawkish and effeminate—the beard, the eyes, the lifted finger of gentle admonishment—and the actual words of the Gospels produced upon me, in another way, much the same effect. I knew such thoughts would be considered sinful with a vengeance, but they remained; and so did that extraordinary feeling of hostility, of a kind of nervous exasperation, which even the playing of a hymn-tune was sufficient to awaken. I hated these hymn-tunes; I hated the words and the music and the instruments associated with them—organs and harmoniums.

What really lay behind this largely instinctive distaste I cannot tell, but I doubt if anything could have eradicated it, and the methods adopted—the compulsory Sunday School and church—were, of course, the least likely to be successful. The doctrine of the Atonement, which had been impressed on me from infancy, struck me as repulsive. Never for a moment did I dream of questioning its truth (I believed all I was taught to believe); it was merely that I did not like it, thought it offensive and humiliating. There was no doubt a grain of arrogance and more than a grain of obstinacy behind such a state of mind, but even had I been utterly docile I do not think the ultimate result would have proved different. At somebody's urgent request I had gone to one of the services which were being held in connection with a Children's Mission (itself an offshoot from a larger evangelistic experiment), and for which a special preacher had come over from England; but this had been the most complete failure of all. I was approached by a furtive she-evangelist named Miss Crouch. Miss Crouch sat down very close beside me—so close that I felt as if I were being embraced—and whispered in my ear that there was to be an after-meeting for which she was sure I should like to wait. She crept noiselessly from pew to pew with these glad tidings, and with intimate questions about one's relations to Jesus. Miss Crouch seemed to me an odious person, and I did not wait for the after-meeting, nor, indeed, for the conclusion of the ordinary service: I left during the temporary disturbance created by somebody having an epileptic fit.

And now the moment Mr. Farrington entered the room I felt uneasy. It was not that I feared lest he too might be subject to fits, but that instantly I became aware of a kind of spiritual emanation—that strange emanation which I hated and fought against, and which I was always aware of in connection with manifestations of religion. I wished my mother, who had brought him up, would remain in the room with us; but she didn't, and he sat down beside my bed, and after the first few words of greeting neither of us said anything.

He seemed to be quite as much at a loss as I was. If I had been older, I dare say it would have been different. As it was, a expect he thought he must approach me in some more youthful and genial spirit than was natural to him: he may even have been aware of my secret antagonism. At last, to break the silence, he took a little book from his pocket and gave it to me, opened, so that I could see my own name written on the end-paper. It was a book of texts—one for each morning of the year—and it was called *Daily Light*. I thanked him for his present, and began to turn the leaves while he, on his part, for lack of anything better to do, lifted the two books lying beside me on the flowered eiderdown, and read their titles aloud. The one in dark green cloth was Miss Broughton's *Doctor Cupid*; the other, a yellow-back, was called *Portia: or By Passions Rocked*. Both had been lent to me by Mrs. Gerrard, who understood my tastes, and Mr. Farrington, who did not, laid them down without comment. At the same moment I laid down *Daily Light*. It was decent of him to have brought it, I thought; but immediately afterwards he rather spoiled this reflection by hoping I should read it, in a tone that implied considerable doubt.

I mumbled some answer, and he began to drum with his fingers on the pictured cover of *Portia*, of which he had again, absent-mindedly, taken possession. I could see that the subtitle was slowly working in, and that he increasingly did not like it. 'By passions rocked!' Sunday after Sunday he preached against allowing oneself to be rocked by passions. Even *Doctor Cupid* he probably suspected of frivolity.

'It seems queer for you to be reading this kind of stuff at your age!' he suddenly began. 'What do you find in it? I'd have thought you'd like adventures or sea stories better—something a little more sensible anyway.'

'I haven't read it yet,' I answered meekly, since he appeared to be referring to *Portia*.

But Mr. Farrington was not satisfied: he looked, indeed, as if he meditated taking both books from me. 'What I object to about rubbish of this kind,' he went on, with an impatient gesture, 'is not so much that there is anything immoral in it (I am sure there isn't, or you wouldn't be allowed to read it), but the calm, self-satisfied way in which it completely *ignores* religion.'

I did not answer, and he turned a sombre and searching gaze upon me. '*Is* religion ever mentioned?' he asked.

'I don't suppose——'

But he did not wait for me to finish. 'And yet the name of God is scattered through these pages.' He had pounced once more on *Doctor Cupid*. 'They might at least leave *Him* out of their foolery.'

I resented this attack, and my dislike of Mr. Farrington increased. It increased still further when he added, in a milder voice, 'Don't you think a fellow ought to do something for his hereafter?'

The phrase jarred on me indescribably. I thought it cheap and common in itself, but the idea behind it I thought particularly ignoble. And it was an idea that both directly and indirectly had been drummed into me over and over again, till I had come to regard it as one of the fundamentals of the Christian ethic. I didn't want a 'hereafter' of the kind Mr. Farrington meant, nor any indeed in which he could possibly share. I wished he would go, and leave me to finish *Doctor Cupid*. But he had no intention of going, and it was only now that he approached what I suppose had been all along the real object of his visit, and began to talk of the illness through which I had passed, and of the mercy that had been shown to me at the last minute. The things he said were irritating, but they were still more surprising. I had never had the slightest thought of dying; nor did I see, if I were doomed to die to-morrow, why he need make such a fuss about it. All this talk of mercy was fiddle-faddle. And how did he know I *wasn't* grateful? Indeed, if it came to that, why should I be more grateful than people who had never been ill at all? It was as if you ought to be grateful to a man who has stuck a knife into you, because he does not finish you outright. This point of view I expressed, and even thought it clever; but such was not Mr. Farrington's opinion. I could see I was producing an unpleasing impression upon him, though he forced a dim smile as he answered, 'You would be thankful to a man who found you lying wounded in the street, and took you home and cured you.'

'Do you mean that it wasn't God who made me ill, but that it was God who made me well?'

I knew he meant nothing of the kind, but he did not speak for a moment or two, and when he did it was only to say, 'I don't think you can realize how ugly words like that sound. Troubles and sicknesses are not sent to us without a purpose. We may not understand the purpose at the time, but sooner or later it is revealed.'

'This one hasn't been revealed yet,' I answered, and immediately regretted my words.

For when the rector had come to see me, before leaving he had knelt down beside the bed and prayed aloud. That was when I was really ill, yet I had not been too ill to feel a pleasant sense of importance. It was quite certain that Mr. Farrington would have prayed also had I shown a different spirit. But now he merely rose from his chair and said good-bye in the ordinary way. And I was disappointed. I wanted a repetition of that scene in which I had been, as it were, the centre of a dramatic struggle between God and the clergy. Mr. Farrington seemed prepared to relinquish me to God. As I clasped his hand all he murmured was a conventional hope that I should soon be better.

I heard him descending the stairs while I reopened *Doctor Cupid*. I was mentally dissatisfied, and I was physically uncomfortable. My pillow had slipped down in the zest of argument, and there was something hard and sharp sticking into my back. What could it be? At any rate, it hurt, for my body was grown abnormally tender. Shifting my position a little, I fumbled rather crossly for the offending object, which at the first touch I recognized. It was *Daily Light*.

XIV

Draw a pail of water
For my lady's daughter;
My father's a King, and my mother's a Queen.
My two little sisters are dressed all in green.
Stamping grass and parsley,
Marigold-leaves and daisies.
One rush—two rush.
I pray thee fine lady come under my bush.

I could see the sunlight shining on the houses opposite; I could see a strip of warm blue sky; I could smell the breath of spring that softly stirred the curtains. . . . And this morning I might get up.

Stamping grass and parsley,
Marigold-leaves and daisies. . . .

The old rhyme kept singing its silly tune in my head, while I wondered if the swallows had taken possession yet of their three round little houses at the back of our house. Year after year they returned to these old nests, exactly like people who have a house in town and a house in the country. Only, imagine flying all the way from Egypt to University Street! Imagine, that is, choosing University Street when one had the wide world to choose from. . . . As soon as I was strong enough I was going on a journey myself—as far as Ballinderry. But then, unlike the swallows, my choice was limited. . . .

With shawls wrapped round me, I might try if I could walk a little—from the bed to Emma's rocking-chair near the window. What nonsense! Of course I could walk quite well:

there was nothing to prevent me from walking: I felt as active as a grasshopper. And then, as I struggled into a sitting position, with my bare legs dangling to the floor, I discovered that I had over-rated my powers a little. I certainly felt more like the careful snail than the impetuous grasshopper. And either my nightshirt had shrunk or my legs had grown unconscionably long. How thin they looked, too! I examined them with a sinking of the heart, and called on my mother, a little querulously, to observe the unpleasing transformation that had taken place. How could I possibly go out in this scarecrow condition? How could I face the stares of other boys? And when she laughed at me I was angry. . . .

But once I was up, though I still seemed to remain abnormally thin, I grew stronger daily. One afternoon I had a visit from a boy who brought me messages from other boys and news of the outside world. I was delighted to see him, but after a few minutes my delight turned to disappointment. We seemed to have nothing to talk about. This was strange, for there were lots of things I wanted to talk about, only they were no longer, somehow, the old things. I realized that I was merely saying what I thought he would expect me to say, and saying it badly, so that he began to fidget and look uncomfortable, and very soon took his departure. When he was gone I felt relieved, yet at the same time vaguely depressed. I was no longer certain of my relation to my old companions. I seemed to have moved mysteriously, either forward or backward: at any rate, my interests were changing, had to a marked extent already changed. . . . Two days later my mother and I left home.

The nearest station to Ballinderry was a forty minutes' journey by a slow train, but the village itself lay in the very heart of the country, and here, at the Glebe, lived Aunt Sarah, and Uncle George (who was also Canon Sayers), in a big white house, standing in fairly extensive grounds.

I am describing the house as it appeared to me then, for I know, from a comparatively recent visit, that it was not really very big. It was low and square, and haunted in summer by a sleepy and continuous music. This music was made by the bees, a whole kingdom of whom had taken up their quarters under the roof and in the roof and all round the roof. Nobody ever dreamed of disturbing them: they were free to eat their own golden store of honey, nor need they fly very far in search of it. Yet they worked from morning till night just the same. There was a hive above my bedroom window and I could hear them buzzing about as soon as I wakened in the morning. Now and then one would stray into the room; but they were not the kind of bees I liked best—not the big, bright, furry bumble bees, which always seemed to me to belong, in some inexplicable way, to the same world as bulldogs, cows, and hippopotamuses.

On one side of the house was a rose garden; on the other a croquet lawn. And there were fruit and vegetable gardens, while the rest of the grounds were left to grow wild.

Uncle George and Aunt Sarah had no children. They lived here alone with two maids, and a cat of remarkable talents named Zoozoo. Zoozoo, when Aunt Sarah had been ill a few years before, had kept her supplied with delicacies in the shape of mice, which he brought in daily, laying them down beside her pillow, sometimes with a kick still left in them, so that she might have the pleasure of killing them herself. Since then he had been credited with every virtue, and was supposed even to refrain from molesting birds. But I was doubtful: the nights were Zoozoo's, and they were long nights, this whole household retiring to rest between half-past nine and ten.

There were one or two men who worked about the place, and who lived in the cottages near by. And in one of the cottages, close to the back gate, there lived a woman whom I was warned by Aunt Sarah not on any account to approach. This warning was given me at lunch a day or two after our arrival, and when Uncle George was not present. Naturally it aroused my curiosity, and I asked why I must not approach her. 'Because she is an undesirable person,' Aunt Sarah answered—a description which, in the event, proved singularly inapt.

I asked why she was undesirable, but Aunt Sarah, with a

meaning glance at my mother, merely said she was not nice. And at once I dropped the subject. Veiled replies, accompanied by glances of secret understanding, I knew well enough to mean that something of a sexual nature was involved, and when Aunt Sarah, speaking guardedly so that it should all pass far beyond my comprehension, told my mother that this woman had 'four sons, all with different surnames, and none with her own surname', the mystery ceased to exist. On a chair between them, with my eyes decorously fixed on my rice pudding and cream, I marvelled a little at the innocence of these two so simple- yet serious-minded ladies. In what world did they imagine I lived? And yet, at the same time, I felt pleased that they should think of me like that—even though it might be rather silly.

As for the person under discussion, my curiosity being satisfied, I forgot all about her. I was much more interested in trying to persuade Uncle George to play croquet with me, a difficult task, because he was nearly always shut up in his study, whither I was forbidden to go. But I had explored the grounds pretty thoroughly by now, and was beginning to be tired of my own company. The spring days were long, and, except the gardeners, there was nobody to talk to. Nor was there any use playing croquet with my mother or Aunt Sarah. They were hopeless, and if I knocked their balls too far away simply made me go and fetch them back again. A game played in this spirit was worse than no game at all.

Aunt Sarah was kind, yet somehow tedious. She fussed too much about my health—far more than my mother did. This was particularly tiresome because there was now nothing the matter with me. But Aunt Sarah wanted me not to run about too much, wanted me to rest after breakfast and after lunch, wanted me not to get overheated, not to catch cold, not to go on the grass till the sun had dried it, not to climb trees, not to walk too far. And what was worst of all, after dinner she wanted to read aloud to me a book called *The Three Tours of Doctor Syntax*. There were plenty of books in the house, and why she should have hit on this, which was not even a story, but a burlesque poem, apparently endless, and written in rhymed doggerel of the dullest description, I cannot conceive. She said it was funny.

> *And when in angry humour talking,*
> *Was like a dumpling set a-walking.*

Lines such as these made Aunt Sarah shake with laughter. As for me, I could have wept from sheer dreariness and vexation of spirit. After the first reading I appealed in private to my mother. But she said Aunt Sarah was reading to me out of kindness, and at any rate couldn't possibly be told not to read.

Why couldn't she be told, I persisted, seeing that her object was kindness?

Because it would hurt her feelings, and her feelings were extremely easily hurt. Nor would it, my mother added, do me any harm to consider now and again other people's enjoyment. A sudden doubt, however, as to my capacity in this direction seemed to assail her, for she gave me a long and steady look. 'Remember, you are not to tell Aunt Sarah you don't like *Doctor Syntax*. It's just the sort of thing you *would* do.'

'I wasn't going to tell her,' I answered sulkily.

'And you're not to let her see you don't like it.'

'How can I help what she sees?'

'If you do anything——' But my mother did not tell me what would happen if I did anything: she wound up by saying that very probably Aunt Sarah herself would get tired of reading.

I knew it wasn't in the least probable, and when *Doctor Syntax* was promptly produced on the following evening I sat down in a chair behind the reader, where I could scowl at my mother as if it were her fault. And this time it was worse than usual, because Aunt Sarah seemed dissatisfied with her audience, or at least with one member of it. Hadn't I any sense of fun, she asked? If *Doctor Syntax* didn't make me laugh, she wondered what would?

The temptation to tell her was irresistible, and I said last night had made me laugh.

'Last night?' Aunt Sarah repeated, not in the least grasping what I meant, nor apparently even remembering what had happened last night. But my mother remembered, for she turned to me with a warning in her eyes which I pretended not to understand.

'When Uncle George got out the telescope to show us the rings of Saturn and we couldn't see anything.'

'But what was funny about that?' Aunt Sarah asked in surprise.

'It was funny when he got crosser and crosser, and then took the telescope away, and banged the study door, and wouldn't come down to supper.'

Well—I had done it, and I waited for what would happen.

Nothing happened: nothing except that Aunt Sarah put away *Doctor Syntax*. I tried to persuade myself that it was all right, and buried my nose in a volume of *Punch*. But when bed-time came I said good-night very sheepishly. My mother did not kiss me. 'I'm ashamed of you,' she whispered; and that was all.

To tell the truth, I was a little ashamed myself. But it was at least the end of *Doctor Syntax*; and from this on I was allowed to choose my own books. I read *This Son of Vulcan*, attracted by the picture on the back, and then I discovered *Tom Sawyer* and *Huckleberry Finn*. The former seemed to me a good story, but the latter was the finest story in the world.

That first reading of *Huck* was one of the most intense pleasures I have ever known. Unfortunately it began just after dinner on a Saturday, and the hour and a half till my bed-time passed like a flash. I was not allowed to take the book upstairs with me, but the moment I had finished breakfast on Sunday morning I ran to the drawing-room to get it. Church was not till twelve, so I had plenty of time for a few chapters. But *Huck* was gone. In the middle of the room was the round walnut table on which I had left him last night, but the only book there now was a book called *The Spanish Brothers*. I rushed to Aunt Sarah to ask her where he was, but my heart sank as I recognized that bright, friendly smile.

'No; *Huck* isn't lost,' she told me cheerfully. 'You'll find he'll be back again on Monday morning. And Uncle George has left *The Spanish Brothers* for you.'

I said not a word: in fact, I retreated hastily so that she might not perceive the extent of my disappointment. I went out by the side door, and discovered that even the croquet hoops had been taken up on Saturday night.

Not that there was anything surprising in this, the same thing having happened on the previous Saturday, only now, because of *Huck*, I regarded the empty lawn with bitterness. Yet nobody would have been more astonished than myself had I come upon a game of croquet actually in progress, for I imagined the conventions in which I had been brought up to be universal laws.

We dined immediately after morning church, so that the servants might have the afternoon free. On this Sunday, when dinner was over, Uncle George went upstairs to his study; Aunt Sarah, my mother, and myself, to the drawing-room, where a fire had been lighted. I would have gone out, but it was raining a little and Aunt Sarah had made a fuss. In a whisper I informed my mother that I wanted *Huckleberry Finn*. I had already mentioned this some dozens of times, so she took no notice. Even *The Spanish Brothers* had now disappeared. I had told Aunt Sarah that I didn't like it, and she had at once—rather unkindly perhaps—taken me at my word, and the book back to Uncle George's study. Later I swallowed my pride sufficiently to ask for it again, but Aunt Sarah said no: Uncle George was busy over his sermon for the evening and mustn't be disturbed. The *Punches*, too, had been cleared away. In fact, so far as I could see, the dazzling choice of entertainment at present before me lay between *The Church Missionary Gleaner* and *The Life of Faith*.

The room was hot, for the mild spring day really made a fire unnecessary. My mother, in one armchair, dozed over *Beyond the Stars*; Aunt Sarah, in another, slept more profoundly, with *God's Everlasting Yea* unopened in her lap. I sat nearer the door. The house was extraordinarily silent; the servants had gone out; Zoozoo had gone out; the kitchen cat had gone out. The contrast between the physical comfort and the spiritual desolation became unendurable. Twice already a sleepy voice had told me not to fidget, but how could I help fidgeting? It seemed to me strange that Aunt Sarah should be so sensible in some ways and so aggravating in others. Her daily habit, for instance, of asking me what kind of puddings I should like cook to make for lunch and dinner was highly commendable. She had a store-room, too, which contained quantities of good things, and she would allow me to help myself to almonds and raisins and preserved ginger and candied fruits, or whatever else I fancied. And my bedroom was delightful, with an armchair, and a little fire if the night happened to be damp or chilly, and sheets and pillow-cases of the finest linen and always faintly smelling of lavender. Here, before I got up in the morning, a beaten-up egg and two raspberry wafers would be brought me; my clothes would be taken away and brushed. It was my first taste of luxury and I enjoyed it.

Yet the time passed slowly. I had nothing to do. There must have been boys of my own age in the neighbourhood, but they were the sons of small farmers and probably already at work: at any rate, I never saw them. And Sunday in the country was just as dreary as Sunday in town. It was worse, for in town I could have gone upstairs and played marbles on the bedroom floor without anybody knowing, or looked over my stamps or my museum. Here there was nothing— this wretched *Gleaner*, with its pictures of half-naked converts—this *Life of Faith*, with *no* pictures—*God's Everlasting Yea*.

I looked out through the window. Against a grey sky the feathery branches of a larch-tree floated, making a delicate pattern. The beauty of the tree pleased me, stirred in me some consoling feeling of fellowship. If only I had been asked to worship and to love the earth I could have done it so easily! If only the earth had been God. The tender green on the trees, the mossy lawns, the yellow daffodils—all these were lovely, and Sunday made no difference to them. Everything seemed to live a natural life on Sundays except people. Cows, birds, cats, dogs, all lived exactly as cows, birds, cats, and dogs had lived from the beginning of the world. It was only people who made difficulties, and thought this was wrong and that was wrong, and did what they didn't enjoy doing. For they *didn't* enjoy it. I had noticed that on Sundays there was an increased irritability even among the most saintly.

My mother was now completely wrapped in slumber. Aunt Sarah, whose head had been nodding lower and lower over her black, beaded bosom, awoke with a slight start and opened her eyes just sufficiently to see that I was still there. She said nothing, however, and presently her eyes closed once more, and again her head began to nod.

I waited for a few minutes. Then I saw that the rain was nearly over and tiptoed from the room. Very gently I opened and shut the hall-door. Nobody could have heard me or I should certainly have been called back to put on an overcoat. As I sped through the wet grass the sun broke from behind the clouds and poured down on my bare head.

The thick mossy grass was softer than a carpet under my feet. There was a little wind, but not much, and it was warm and scented. There were daffodils, and where the trees were not already clothed with green their branches were covered with buds. The rhododendrons were covered with buds, too, moist and sticky and bursting with life. Life was everywhere —in the insects, in the birds—colour, joy, ecstasy, music, the mystery of procreation, the mystery of growth and growing things, a kind of intoxication that came with the wind, the scent of flowers and shrubs and grasses, the heat of the sun; and I felt it all thrilling in my own blood as I lifted my head and shook the raindrops down from a dark cedar branch over my face and throat, while my skin tingled deliciously at the wet, cool little touches. It was the rapturous fermentation of spring that I felt, swelling and bursting, piercing up through the brown earth, breaking into flower—breaking into a flame of intense blue that burned and blazed and splashed all over the lush green of the deeper hollows. I drew the air far down into my lungs and raised my voice in my own kind of hymn.

It was apparently a kind understood by someone else, for

a much louder, harsher voice was raised in antiphon. I knew the ancient joke that a third person would have made. Then my solitary playmate came galloping over the grass—a stiff, lumbering gallop, for the years had begun to weigh upon him, and only his tail remained as frisky as of yore. His grey coat was as thick as a doormat and as dusty, and of all those I have ever met he was the fondest of company. While I remained in his part of the grounds he followed me closer than a dog, so close, indeed, that the only comfortable way to walk was to put my arm round his shoulder exactly as Alan used to do with me. It was in this fashion that we now proceeded half round the field, till we reached a hillock from which, through the trees, I caught sight of the road and of a cottage whose chimney sent a wisp of smoke blowing out across the dappled sky. It was the cottage I had been warned against, as if it were a witch's house in a fairy tale. I stood gazing at it, while gradually the idea formed in my mind that this would be a good opportunity to try to catch a glimpse of the witch herself.

I bid a temporary farewell to my companion, climbed a railing, and ran down the slope to where there was a gap in the hedge, through which I peered. She was there, had just come out with a wooden bucket which she carried round to fill from a well at the side of the cottage. I could hear the clanking of the handle and the splash of water. I could see her quite plainly, a stoutish woman, but not fat; dark-skinned like a Spaniard, with greying hair, dark bright eyes, and a pleasant mouth. A sudden impulse seized me and I crept through the hedge and out on to the road. I was standing there straight in front of the little green gate when she returned with the slopping, brimming pail, and when I smiled at her she smiled back again. I was not very thirsty but I thought I would ask for a drink, and somehow, before I thoroughly realized what was happening, I was in the kitchen, seated on a chair in the chimney-corner, and a shaggy, nondescript dog was stuffing a moist cold nose into my hand. There was a cat too, and there were pots of geraniums in the window, and on the wall a picture of Christian saying good-bye to his wife and family, and lots of blue and gold and pink and white china ornaments, and a pleasant smell of freshly baked bread over everything. I had a slice of hot soda-bread and butter and a cup of milk, and I learned that the dog's name was Tramp, because he had been a stray dog. The cat, like the Glebe kitchen cat, had never been christened. As for my own name, which I volunteered, she knew it already, and apparently everything else about me, even that I had been ill. Seeing she knew so much I described my illness, and told her how thin it had made me, but that now I was getting all right again. She dug her finger softly into my cheek, and felt my arms and legs, and thought they still weren't much to boast of. This performance made me laugh. It was not a bit the way a doctor examined you, nor the way Aunt Sarah fussed. I liked her, I had liked her from the very first moment: her hands were strong yet gentle, and I liked her colour and her eyes and her mouth. If I had ever seen pictures by Frans Hals I probably should have thought she was not unlike a woman he might have painted. At any rate, I felt much happier in this kitchen, with its cat and its dog, than I had felt in the drawing-room at the Glebe half an hour ago.

For a few minutes she moved about, putting things away, making up the fire; then she sat down on the opposite side of the hearth, and Tramp instantly forsook me and lay down at her feet. And now, I must confess, a rather odd thing happened (odd because I was getting to be a fairly big boy and as a rule was shy with strangers). But I felt a sudden desire to go and sit on her knee. I wished she would ask me to do so, but she didn't; I wished that I was smaller so that I might have invited myself, but I remained the same size. And I could not help remembering certain drives I had taken. I wanted her to put her arms round me: I wanted her, above all, to *want* to do it, to be enthusiastic, like the poultry woman. The cat had jumped into her lap; Tramp was as close to her as he could possibly get; and somehow my distance of a yard or two seemed to isolate me, to shut me out in the cold. I slipped down off my seat and pretended to admire the geraniums in the window. From the geraniums I turned to an examination of the china figures in a dresser which stood against the wall just beyond her chair. I was touching the side of the chair now, leaning over it, and presently, whether she drew me on to her knee, or whether I simply got there myself, I don't know, but I know that I *was* there, and that her arms were round me, encompassing me in that close bodily contact I loved.

She smelt nice; she smelt of the bread she had been baking; and her brown and ruddy skin was smooth yet not too smooth, but velvety, like the skin of a peach or an apricot. I lay in luxurious stillness, all my limbs relaxed and perfectly at ease, as if I were lying in a warm bath, or had only half awakened out of sleep. And when she caressed me exactly the way one would caress an animal, her hand drawing in a slow rhythmic sweep down my side from shoulder to knee, I felt strange little electric thrills passing through my body, and queer little noises rising in my throat—noises which I only half suppressed, so that she laughed and said I was a fox and knew how to get what I wanted.

I liked her to call me a fox. I liked everything about her. She stopped stroking me, but I whispered to her to go on, and burying my face in the softness of her throat I pressed against her, while a deep strange pleasure passed through me in waves, like the ripples in water. But suddenly she pulled my flushed face up and looked straight into my eyes. Then she kissed me on the mouth. 'Now; that's all the petting you're going to get, my fine fellow,' she said, and I hid my cheek against her shoulder but did not answer.

The rapidity with which this intimacy had been established did not strike me as surprising. Had I not often myself established equally swift relations with dogs or other animals, and this was in its nature very much akin to them, was, at any rate, a thing entirely independent of speech. As I still lay there in her arms I had a momentary vision of the drawing-room at the Glebe, and knew that by this time I must certainly have been missed. But I did not let the thought disturb me—all that could be dealt with later. How long, indeed, I should have been prepared to remain I cannot tell: it was

Anna herself (for that was her name), who presently told me I had better be going back. I slid off her knee, still without saying anything; but I did not want to go, I hovered beside the chair. Then I heard the clicking of a latch, a step on the gravel outside, a heavier step that paused on the kitchen threshold. The sturdy, pleasant-faced youth who helped the gardener at the Glebe stood there, his mouth widened to a broad grin. I had forgotten all about the four mysterious sons. Here evidently was one of them. And to find that it was Jim, who actually worked for Uncle George! He looked from me to his mother, and continued to smile a little shyly. For some reason I too felt shy.

'Why don't you say good evening?' his mother asked Jim rather sharply, and he obediently repeated the words. I too repeated them.

He had come in for his tea, Jim added, so I knew there was nothing left for me to do but say good-bye. Yet I half hoped they would ask me to have tea with them. I wanted to stay, though I knew that every five minutes would add to my difficulties when I got back. Indeed, if questioned closely, I was lost. I could deceive by remaining silent, but to tell a direct lie I found impossible. It was somehow against the grain—against my grain—and I couldn't do it. However, I was not asked to stay. I left without even an allusion having been made to any future visits. I should surely come again, I thought, but it did not matter. The whole adventure was entirely free from sentiment, was merely something pleasant that had happened. And for all my perturbation as to what might await me there, I sped home happily through the windy evening glow.

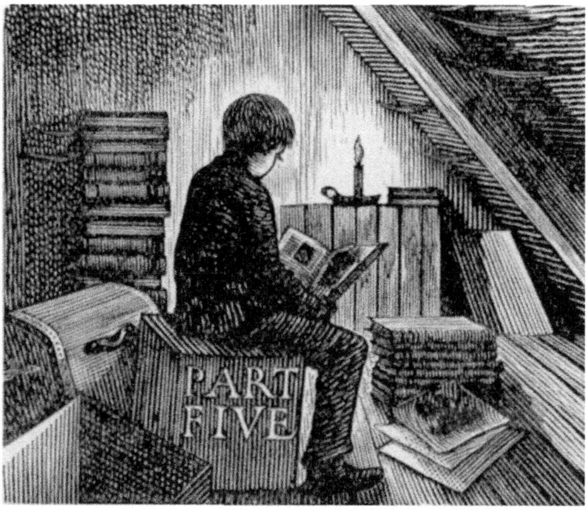
PART
FIVE

XV

I was seated at a table turning over the engravings of Holbein's *Dance of Death* when Professor Park entered. The room was his study, and I had called to borrow *Faust*.

I had not, up till the present, been very successful with the classics. I had failed badly with *Don Quixote* and the *Morte d'Arthur*, getting not a quarter way through the first volume of either of them; I had been even less successful with *The Divine Comedy*; but I was ready to go on trying, though who or what had put me on the track of *Faust* I cannot now remember.

At any rate, the volume Professor Park placed in my hands was of no use to me. It was in German and I told him I couldn't read German. He thought for a moment and then suggested Marlowe, at the same time taking down a fat, dowdy-looking book from an upper shelf. Its letterpress, when I opened it, was no more attractive than its binding; it was printed in double columns, a form I have always disliked and found difficult to read; but it contained *The tragicall History of Doctor Faustus*. It also contained, as I discovered on the following Sunday afternoon, a poem called *Hero and Leander*, a poem for which I quickly deserted *Doctor Faustus*, a poem which I re-read on many a succeeding Sunday, until I came to regard it as a kind of antidote to the normal effects of that sacred day.

Now I had my book I might of course have departed, but I made no attempt to do so. And presently I was listening to a dissertation on the German genius, which passed, I know not how, into an examination of the human taste for marvels, for tales of witches and warlocks, vampires, werewolves, fairies, ghouls, salamanders. Since I shared this taste to a marked degree myself, I was deeply interested in it. I heard how it had been exploited in past ages by wizards and charlatans, and how it was still exploited by their descendants; I heard anecdotes of Professor Park's own adventures among such persons, and the beginning of a ghost story which, for some reason, he decided not to finish. I was rather glad he didn't finish it; the beginning was filled with the most disquieting circumstantiality; but I sat entranced. It was exactly the kind of talk I liked, and the kind of talk I never got from anybody else. Not adapted to my years (except, I suppose, in this matter of ghosts), assuming, rather, that there existed between us an equality of intelligence, and even of experience, it had the effect of making me intelligent, of making me feel I was taking part in the discussion. This feeling was produced by the courteousness with which he weighed my own small contributions, trying to make the most of them, developing them, indeed, till I wondered how I could have thought of anything half so clever. It was this that made his company so agreeable; this, perhaps, that made me think we had so much in common. And yet, from past disappointments, I knew, too, that our pleasant relationship would end as soon as I had said good-bye. Here was the secret of my discontent. I never seemed to make any progress. It was as if each time we met I entered his field of consciousness as a fresh phenomenon, and there were moments even now, while he gazed beyond me and out of the window, when I had an uneasy sense of insubstantiality, as if I were already melting into the figment of his dream. His voice would die away to a whisper that caressed some last word upon the wings of which his imagination had taken flight into incommunicable regions—regions, at all events, whither I could not follow him. It was as if he had been holding my hand as we threaded together the winding paths of a labyrinth, and then had suddenly let go. The next moment he was round the corner, lost to sight, and I was alone between the high thick hedges. I did not like this feeling, this feeling of being abandoned, forgotten; it produced upon me a chilling effect. I called after him, but no answer came; he was gone; there was not even an echo from my own voice; there was nothing but an empty silence. The instant his study door closed behind me, I knew I should cease to exist for him, should fade out as rapidly as a breath from a glass; and at our next encounter we would have to begin all over again. It was a pity. I still think it a pity—so far as I was concerned—and a loss. For if I had no other virtues I was at least responsive, and my mind was receptive and sensitive. I admired him, too, with the wholehearted enthusiasm of boyhood. He went out for a lonely walk each afternoon, and at the slightest hint that loneliness might have been avoided. But the hint never came.

I sometimes wondered *why* it never came. The simple, if distressing explanation, that I was rather a little bore, did not occur to me. It is not an explanation that ever occurs to a child. It is one of the joyous discoveries of the middle years. But what most astonished me was the fact that neither of his own two boys showed the least desire to share his rambles. Nor did they, as I fancied I did, share his tastes. I shared them to such an extent that I was prepared to take an interest even in the subjects he lectured on, logic and metaphysics. It is true, my conception of these subjects was vague, and, since nobody seemed willing to enlighten me, it remained vague. Logic, according to my mother, meant 'proving things': metaphysics meant 'philosophy': but these definitions I found unsatisfying. I knew that metaphysics had to do with the propounding of mysterious riddles concerning time and space and matter—riddles at the nature of which I could not so much as guess. I had myself tried to grasp the notion of time, but the effort produced a sickening, rather frightening feeling, because I could only imagine it as relative to myself, to my present life and what had led up to it. I could only think in a circle; if I tried to project my mind along a straight line, and to carry that line on to infinity, it became a nightmare. What Professor Park's philosophy was I did not know, though I thought it was derived from the Germans, and knew that among modern philosophers he was most in sympathy with Bradley, with whom, indeed, he corresponded. Bradley, he had once told me, was a pessimist, so I supposed he was a pessimist too. But all this had little meaning; and what I actually knew was that he was gentle and melancholy, a grey little man, dressed in grey, who carried his head on one side and walked very close to the kerb-stone, and possessed a mind that was of the most absorbing interest. Nobody else I knew seemed to possess a mind at all. If they did, they kept its workings and discoveries to themselves.

One afternoon I encountered Professor Park by chance in the Linen Hall Library, and mentioned to him my incomplete knowledge of German philosophy. I had not spoken to him for a long time, though by religiously taking off my cap when I met him in the street, I had kept up a bowing acquaintance. But I did not meet him very often now, because he had left Mount Charles and gone to live in University Square. I was not even sure that he would remember my name; I was not sure, indeed, that he had ever known it, or whether I had ever been anything more than merely the boy next door. You see, there was nothing to *tell* me he knew me: he would have bowed to anyone who took off his cap. Of course, I now feel certain he was a great deal more like other people than I believed him to be, and that he knew all about me; but at that time I really was as doubtful as I say; and this in spite of the friendliness with which he invariably received me—after I had taken the first step. Nothing, for instance, could have been more encouraging than his manner on that afternoon. He had been sitting down, turning over the pages of a review, but the moment I spoke he got up, and with his hand on my shoulder piloted me to a window, in the recess of which we could converse. His voice, after a minute or two, was as usual lowered to a pitch which suggested that what we were saying had better be kept strictly between ourselves. In other words, we both talked in hoarse whispers, for that was his way, and after a little I would catch it from him. To a third person we must have presented the oddest appearance, as of an ill-assorted brace of conspirators plotting deeds of darkness. An occasional straggler, looking for a book on the nearer shelves, would give us in passing a glance of curiosity. What were we up to? that glance seemed to wonder. And to tell the truth I didn't quite know myself. But we had a serious question to decide and we approached it literally with bated breath. What should I read? I could never have guessed beforehand that it mattered so much as this. Apparently the weightiest issues were at stake. I could not help feeling that I was being taken more seriously than I deserved, and that I ought to tell him of the diversity of my interests, which seemed to be pulling me in countless directions at the same time, and of how subject I was to violent enthusiasms, and how invariably my desires outran achievement.

On the whole, probably, the book that would give me the best bird's-eye view of German philosophy was *The Veil of Isis*. I had read Kant, of course? No: I hadn't read Kant—though I was by this time almost ashamed to admit it. And indeed the admission seemed to be disappointing, and in a single instant, I could see, increased our difficulties tenfold. Here was a boy of fourteen who hadn't read Kant! I felt the next question ought to be, What can we do with him? I said I had thought of reading Bradley's *Appearance and Reality*, but even for that, it seemed, I must read Kant first. Kant was now a roaring lion in our path, and somehow, though for no better reason than that he appeared to be so necessary, I conceived a dislike for him. He sounded dry; he sounded mathematical, cold, forbidding. I could make a beginning with English philosophy, Professor Park said, and this I should find all plain sailing. I might read Berkeley, or perhaps Spencer's *First Principles*. But I knew at once that these were not the real thing; were a compromise. I would read Kant, since I was obliged to read him; I would take home the *Critique of Pure Reason* that evening; and Professor Park admitted this perhaps would be best; certainly it must be done before I could think of tackling Hegel's *Logic*. And I had better read Wallace on Hegel: Wallace was remarkably lucid, and the *Logic* was not an easy book.

Now that we had reached a decision our talk gradually became more general; we wandered hither and thither over the ground—to me a strange, twilit landscape, through whose shadows there loomed mountain peaks bearing unfamiliar names—Fichte, Schelling, Lotze, Wundt, Hartmann, Schopenhauer. Before long I had mapped out a course of reading which would last me for the remainder of my days.

Professor Park looked out softly into the fading November street, and I looked out too. We stood there, wrapped in the encroaching darkness, thousands of miles from the people coming and going with novels under their arms, from the people in arm-chairs reading magazines and newspapers, from the people passing under the town lamps, which were gleaming out one by one, like stars at the waving of a magician's wand. The magician was only the hurrying lamplighter who, as he passed, changed the scene from day to night. The lights in the library had been lit some time ago, but they did not penetrate to our recess, and it was in the pallid half-light of the outside world that I saw Professor Park's colourless, rather small face, his straight thin silvery hair, his narrow stooping shoulders, his thin hands. An indescribable sadness seemed all in a moment to have fallen upon him. He reminded me, I don't quite know how, of an old grey horse I had once seen standing solitary and motionless in a field at nightfall. There was the same mildness, the same innocence, the same expression of an immemorial patience.

And these qualities produced upon me their inevitable effect. I was seized with an intense desire to act as comforter—to murmur little words, to pat and stroke and caress. But presently I stole away, for I knew the conversation was ended, and that his thoughts were no longer communicating with mine, though on what secret quest they had flown out I could not tell.

XVI

I don't think, in spite of my mother's suggestion, it can really have been the ghost of Uncle Henry who urged me, even in those early days, to 'collect'. If it was, how he must have wept over my collections; and Professor Park's were not much better. He collected fossils, butterflies, and autographs; but perhaps, so far as the sport is concerned, it does not much matter what is collected.

For it *is* a sport; and though the 'bag' be no more than a heap of old cookery-books, or a cupboard-load of pamphlets printed in one's native town, yet just as much as for those who leave a trail of dead and wounded creatures behind them when they tramp the woods with a gun, the pleasure here, too, lies mainly in the chase. No book looks so well when you have catalogued it and placed it on its appointed shelf as it did in the dusty little shop where you first unearthed it; and the collector, like other lovers, need expect no permanent rapture. Possession will dull his zest; his passion will decline to affection; he may even prove unfaithful and follow vagrant loves; certainly the first fine thrill of discovery can never be recaptured.

Yet his hobby, whatever it be, does add a vast enjoyment to life. And when the time comes for him to seek the auction rooms of Paradise that enjoyment is, as it were, released, like the sun's heat from a burning coal, and spreading out into the air, generates excitement, conjecture, a pleasant flutter of catalogue leaves, a condition, in short, which is as far removed as possible from the depressing stagnation that usually accompanies death. . . .

Needless to say, it was not of books, nor indeed of any objects possessing either an aesthetic or commercial value, that my first collections were composed. They were no better than the pickings of ash-pits; I was no better than a little rag-and-bone man. I collected matches, for instance. I doubt if most people suspect there are twenty varieties of matches in the world; but I knew there were more, far more, and I pursued them quietly, but with a marvellous concentration of purpose. Calamity, swift and spectacular, overtook this particular collection, which 'passed away in one high funeral gleam' more rapidly than Troy Town. On a Monday morning, with the intention of throwing it open to the public, I brought it to school in my trousers pockets. A dangerous place wherein to carry loose matches; but then, I had no other pockets, my upper garment being a blue jersey. Naturally, every now and again I felt to see if my matches were all right, and it was while I was doing so, and during a recital of the books of the Bible, that they suddenly ignited with a startling effect. Mabel Johnston, who was sitting next me, screamed; I grew as red as a turkey-cock; but Miss Hardy understood that it had been an accident, and telling Mabel not to be silly, dismissed me to the lavatory to examine more closely into my damages.

My collection of nibs was just as stupid, and so were my collections of puzzles, of stamps, of wallpapers (perhaps the most idiotic of all), of posters (for though these latter may have looked well enough on hoardings, they were so big that when I had pasted the parts together I had to keep them wrapped round a pole). And yet (such is the sheepishness of human nature), all these crazes, except that of the posters, spread through the school like mumps or measles.

It was Professor Park who, with a boxful of rubbish from his own overflowing heap, and a discarded butterfly net, turned me to less innocent pursuits. On his drawing-room chimney-piece was a large gilt clock under a glass shade, and this clock was covered with dead butterflies. It represented, I imagine, his sole experiment in artistic expression, and though it fascinated me, I did not regard it as successful. Nevertheless, I too became a butterfly hunter, and a little later started a museum. I cleaned out a large press built into the wall of my bedroom, and here improved the shining hours by arranging and rearranging a dismal hoard of objects. I had covered the shelves with a layer of fine sea sand to the depth of about an inch, and on this I laid out my spoils. Unfortunately, though lavish with fossils and birds' eggs, Professor Park had given me no skeletons, and skeletons were essential. To obtain a couple I buried a dead rat and a largish fish, and afterwards dug them up, a stomach-turning task, because, as might have been expected, I dug them up a great deal too soon. Moreover, even without skeletons, my bedroom (which was not unshared) had by this time acquired a distinctive atmosphere; and one day, after neglecting the museum for a week or two, I unlocked its doors to discover I had now not only dead but living specimens. It was the end; I quailed before the task that faced me; a sulky maid was summoned, and the museum transported to the ash-pit.

It was in a much less ardent spirit that I started an aquarium, and when most of the inhabitants developed legs and wings and a marked distaste for what I had believed to be their native element, I accepted this second slap of fortune with resignation. For a day or two our house was very like Eden, filled with a busy and harmonious humming, which was pierced every now and again by a scream from one or other of my sisters when some fat and friendly beetle alit for a moment on her head; but I was forbidden further experiments, nor did I particularly wish to try them. I was not, I found, cut out to be a naturalist. Dead things distressed me, and living things in bowls or cages distressed me even more. I had always had qualms about butterfly hunting, qualms about bird's-nesting, and, contrary to the laws of psychology, custom did not remove them. I had seen a moth which I had shaken out from my 'killing bottle' apparently dead—which I had indeed mounted on a card, and labelled—coming to life an hour later, and promenading round the glass-lidded case with a pin still thrust through his thick hairy body. The sight filled me with horror, and completed my disgust for this kind of entomology.

There followed, I suppose, a lull in my activities; it was, at any rate, a year or two later, when I must have been fifteen, that they received a fresh stimulus, and one which, because it jumped with my own interests and inclinations, was to prove more satisfying.

I had been prowling on a wet afternoon backwards and forwards between the kitchen and the parlour, having nothing else to do. Everybody seemed cross and disobliging. My sisters had refused to play cards with me; my mother had refused to give me butter and sugar to make toffee. I went upstairs to the drawing-room and improvised on the piano for a few minutes, till a not unexpected message reached me that I was either to play properly or to stop playing. I shut the piano and ascended still higher; in fact, to the very top landing, off which opened the servant's bedroom, my own bedroom, and the lumber-room. This last was an attic full of big trunks, broken furniture, old books, old clothes, and odds and ends of all sorts. It had a queer smell as I entered and closed the door behind me—a dry and slightly bitter smell, which was composed of the smells of cloth and leather and wood and paper and dust. I opened one of the boxes and the smell became intensified, and at the same time different, being mingled with an odour of camphor. I lifted out a tray of silks and ribbons, and the first thing I found underneath was a dress-suit which I knew must have belonged to my father. Before a cracked and foggy mirror I arrayed myself in this, but the trousers felt cold against my legs as I buttoned them round me, and when I postured in front of the ancient glass I became conscious of a strange and slightly ghostly sensation, not quite agreeable, and yet not strong enough to make me desist. In moving I had displaced a stack of magazines, some of which had slid to the floor. I now noticed that one of them lay open, showing a woodcut that caught my attention. The paper was toned to an ivory yellow; the design showed a little harbour with a woman and a child walking by the water's edge, and a man standing on the wharf, holding a bag on a truck. In the background were the black naked ropes and masts and spars of the boats, and the whole thing seemed to me charming.

There and then, under the sunless pallor of the skylight,

I sat down and looked for other drawings. There were plenty, for there were heaps of these old magazines—*Good Words, Cornhills, Quivers, Argosys, Once a Weeks*. To me they were treasure trove. I had never been in a picture gallery in my life (because there was none in my native town): with the exceptions of Millais, and Holman Hunt, and such old *Punch* friends as du Maurier and C. K., I had never heard of the artists over whose work I now pored. Nor was my pleasure lessened when in a flash I saw here the nucleus of a new collection—a real collection this time, not a mere accumulation of rubbish. In a remarkably few minutes I had changed back into my own clothes, but not before my original plan of rushing downstairs to ask my mother to give me these magazines had had time to appear over sanguine. She would ask me what I wanted them for, and when I said I wanted the pictures would tell me I could look at them as often as I liked. Even if she gave them to me she would still desire to know what I was going to do with them, and at the first mention of scissors there would be an end of my collection. She would not understand my purpose, and would regard it as mere destructiveness. She would be backed up by my sisters too, who would be sure to suggest a hospital, or the Deaf and Dumb Institution, or something of the kind. The suggestion would not be prompted by the least interest in the deaf and dumb, nor would the deaf and dumb be the least interested in Pinwell's drawings; but all the same they would get them. It would be better not even to borrow the scissors, I now saw, or rather not to mention I was borrowing them. Once I had my pictures ready, the secret would have to be revealed, for I could not mount them up here where there was no table; but I did not dwell on this, I thought only of the hours and days of enjoyment before me. So I slipped downstairs for the scissors, and without further ado settled to my task.

In the lumber-room it was cold, for these were October days, and it would have been nicer to have worked on the hearthrug in front of the dining-room fire, and under the benevolent supervision of Tabby's successor; but I durstn't risk it, so I worked on a low wooden box under the skylight, and when it became too dark to see I lit a candle. The candle shed a forlorn light across the mingle-mangle of variegated litter, creating shadows which were out of all proportion black and solid. Not a sound reached me, not a sound in the candle-lit stillness but the rustle of paper and the snip-snip of my scissors. There had been a time when I should not have sat here quite so tranquilly, I thought; for lumber-rooms were well known to be dubious places, attractive to the ghostly owners of the shrouded spoils they held. As, decked in my father's clothes, I had mimed and preened myself in front of that cracked mirror, subconsciously, and not so very subconsciously perhaps, it had really been the notion that his face might peep over my shoulder which had made me uneasy. But there was nothing in such moon-and-green-cheese stuff, I now told myself, and, though the fact that it should have occurred to me at all rather contradicted this bold intellectual scepticism, I worked on in my den—a thought uneasily it may be—till the ringing of a bell called me down to light and warmth and the cheerful noise of a large family gathered round a tea-table.

Tea was by far the pleasantest meal of the day; at least, it was the one I most enjoyed. Breakfast was usually a scramble against time; my dinner, except on Saturdays and Sundays, I had by myself; but at tea everybody was present, and there would be an air of general relaxation and jollity. But principally I liked these tea gatherings because my sister Fanny, when she wished to do so, could always make me roar with laughter, and my own sallies came in well enough, though they were not nearly so sustained as hers. She had several character parts which appeared to me irresistible. Home-brewed jokes, requiring their own setting, their own atmosphere, neither very brilliant nor very subtle, well-worn indeed and comfortable as old slippers, nevertheless they were of the kind I liked, and somehow still like, best.

Meanwhile, in the black-and-white art of the 'sixties I became from day to day more deeply versed. Pinwell (my first discovery), Boyd Houghton, Fred Walker, J. D. Watson,

Sandys, North, Arthur Hughes—these and others were names very soon as familiar to me as my own. And C. K., who had always been my favourite, whose jokes were better than anybody else's, turned out to be Charles Keene, who could make beautiful drawings as well as comic ones. The majority of the designs were illustrations for serial stories. There were William Small's drawings for *Griffith Gaunt*; du Maurier's for *Eleanor's Victory*, *Foul Play*, and *Wives and Daughters*; Charles Keene's for *A Good Fight* and *Evan Harrington*; Millais's and Fred Walker's for the tales of Miss Martineau and the novels of Trollope; Pinwell's and Arthur Hughes's for stories by George Macdonald. These woodcuts possessed an increasing fascination for me. They accepted life as it was and turned it into beauty; they invested the most homely material with a delicate and poetic charm.

So I cut out and mounted my pictures, carefully dating each drawing, and writing its title at the foot of the board, and the title of the magazine in which I had found it. My collection began to grow bulky, though it was limited to the spoils of the lumber-room. As for those volumes which I saw priced at a few pence on second-hand-book stalls—I had no money to buy one of them.

XVII

My singing voice had begun to break on the upper notes (I could no longer take even a G with security), though I continued to sing, or rather to make a noise, with the result that in after years I was unable to sing at all. But this result was perhaps not entirely due to the strain I put upon my voice; I fancy Doctor Walton Brown had also a little to do with it. From childhood I had suffered a lot from sore throats, and now, one of these attacks having been complicated by a sudden deafness, Doctor Brown was consulted, and declared I should have been sent to him long ago. He undertook, at all events, to remove the weakness for ever, and he succeeded, but by methods so drastic that not even the voice of a young Tita Ruffo could have survived them. He was a surgeon of the old school, a tall and extremely handsome man, though of a somewhat cold and, to me, unsympathetic type. In his manner he was genial, with a dash of brutality and very little patience. Some of his female visitors he terrified nearly out of their wits, and he used to damn them freely after their departure. The men he damned to their faces. Thus schooled, I was as alert and obedient as a soldier on parade, and was proud of the fact that I never had to be sworn at. On the contrary, with a half-ironic twinkle in his eyes he would give me a word of praise and a pat on the shoulder when we said good-bye. I used to go to him immediately after school (he lived within a stone's-throw of the gates), but though I arrived at about five minutes past three he invariably kept me waiting till he had attended to all his other patients first—that is to say, till about half-past five or six.

There was another boy whom I now and then saw there. I never spoke to him because he was always with his mother, and I forget, though the doctor told me at the time, what was the matter with him. One side of his face was covered with sticking-plaster, and because he used to cry when this plaster was torn off his cheek (and I am sure it was literally torn off), and because his mother insisted on going into the room with him, the doctor detested them both. 'These damned women!' he would say. 'Drink tea till their nerves are in rags, and then come here and make a scene about their brats.' Streaming with blood through my mouth and nostrils, it was all very well to be assured that he liked a boy who wasn't afraid of a little pain; but in reality I was just as much afraid of it as anybody. His remarks had the effect of making me pretend I wasn't—since I could usually pump up a virtue I was given credit for—nevertheless, one afternoon the world grew dark before my eyes, and I collapsed on the floor—a weakness which filled me with shame.

Doctor Brown did not believe in anaesthetics. First he removed my tonsils, a not very serious matter, especially when one is told that that will be all. But on my next visit I found it was only the beginning. It had been a simple operation—clean, neat, rapid, and accomplished with an instrument: the subsequent performances were less conventional. It is true an instrument (even several of them) would be there; but after the briefest trial it would be consigned to the lower world and the doctor would use his fingers. How much of my throat he tore away in this fashion I don't know, but I should think a considerable portion. Besides the pain, there was the horrible messiness of it, and the fact that the task seemed endless. Each day when I got my encouraging pat I would be told he had finished, that the next appointment was merely to see how the torn places had healed. False promises! There was always more to be done; and there were always, before it *was* done, those dismal hours of waiting, only faintly solaced by a couple of Persian cats. The other boy would come in an hour after me, but would be taken before me, and I would be left with my cats. Then, when all was over, with my bag of school-books and three or four bloody pocket-handkerchiefs, I would return home in the tram. Yet, though the method was rough, it was successful, and the memory of those visits comes back to me now as incredibly mingled with a kind of hard gaiety—my generalized impression, I suppose, of all the forgotten stories I was told to keep up my spirits. The actual work would be accompanied by a soothing flow of profanity from the lips of the operator, in which the half-strangled patient would gladly have joined; and the doctor, though he made many jokes about my cheque-book, neither then nor later would accept a fee.

Meanwhile all the arts seemed to be tugging at me simultaneously. It was a period of enthusiasm, of rapture, of discovery. Emotionally I lived in a state of perpetual simmering, which every now and again boiled over, as when I first heard the music of Richard Wagner and of Hector Berlioz.

My literary discoveries were sometimes less happy. It could hardly have been otherwise, since I was exploring an absolutely unknown sea, and had no friendly pilot to drop me a hint, while the rudder of a very young and untrained taste was apt to play me strange pranks.

I dare say it played me such a prank in that hour when I chanced on a copy of Miss Corelli's *Ardath*, and was straightway rapt by it into the seventh heaven of romantic poetry. Not that I accepted *Ardath* in its entirety. I have not looked at the book since, but I remember that the last part of it, when the hero suddenly finds himself back in the modern world, seemed to me then so bad that it weakened the impression of what had gone before. Yet that impression still remains. It is of a man, a solitary traveller, wandering among the wild cliffs and passes of a range of eastern mountains. A tremendous storm arises, the sky is darkened, day is turned into night, the winds howl, the rain sweeps down in torrents, he is lost. But still he struggles on, fighting for life. And at last he reaches an unknown monastery built on the mountain side, and there finds a refuge. He comes in from the darkness and the tempest, from the rain and snow and wind and ice, to the warmth of a lighted chapel where the monks are chanting the Magnificat. When the service is over, they ask him to remain as their guest. But in the middle of the night, being unable to sleep, he goes out, and climbs down into the plain. The storm has passed; there is a strange white stillness over the earth; the moon is floating in a black sky, and a pale lunary radiance floods the desolate land in which he finds himself. It is the field of Ardath, 'the field of flowers, where no house is builded', to which the Angel Uriel sent Esdras after he had fasted for seven days, telling him to eat only of the flowers. The Wanderer plucks a white flower growing in the grass and eats it. And as he does so the scene around him drifts away, a harsh sun bursts out of the sky, and he finds himself at the gate of a city. The streets are full of colour and din; white towers and minarets glitter in the sunshine; and when the Wanderer looks down he sees that he is clothed as the other men in the city are. He remembers the city, he knows its narrow twisted streets; it is Al Kyris, older than Babylon, beautiful and evil as the Cities of the Plain. And he is plunged back into a life he has already lived, a life gorgeous and perilous as an Arabian tale, but ending in a terrific cataclysm that brings the whole city toppling down like a house of cards.

Such was the tale of *Ardath*—a thing of overwhelming wonder and fascination, rich and romantic as the poetry of Keats, and far more exciting. Can I read *any* book to-day with just that complete absorption in it? I think not. What I got then probably was the *Ardath* of Miss Corelli's conception; what I should get now would be the very much less splendid *Ardath* of her actual achievement. Its gorgeousness would all too likely strike me as vulgarity, its passionate adventure as melodrama, its poetry as a crude straining after effect. But is this so great a boon in a world where splendid achievements are rare? Might it not be argued that in any work of art it is the emotion awakened by it that matters? Why should I consider the pleasure I now receive from *The Spoils of Poynton* or *L'Éducation Sentimentale* or *La Rôtisserie de la Reine Pédauque* to be more valuable than the pleasure I received in those days from *Ardath*? It is not so intense; it does not make me hold my breath; it does not set my nerves and senses tingling. Nor is there much use, with my recollection of it, pretending that the old pleasure was not an aesthetic pleasure at all. It was. That is the whole point. It filled my mind with beauty. A barbaric, apocalyptic beauty I dare say —streaked with lust and blood and flaming strident colours —but still beauty. The whole question leaves me dubious.

Ardath was written in prose, with, I suspect, a liberal sprinkling of blank verse, for this, in the only book on Miss Corelli's art that has yet appeared, is mentioned as a feature of her style. More: it is mentioned as a beautiful feature. Well—why not? It would be a poor thing to sneer at effects that once enthralled me. Verse rhythms probably abounded in my own earliest efforts; I certainly tried to get a regular, measured beat, a fullness of sound that I could read in a kind of chant.

As a matter of fact, an appreciation of prose, as prose, usually, I fancy, comes later than an appreciation of verse. This is natural, because the music of prose is so much less emphatic than the music of verse. Be it as it may, my own taste in poetry underwent no such remarkable transformation as my taste in prose. The kind of poetry I like best now I liked then; much of the prose I liked then I could not now read without discomfort. In poetry there were three qualities I looked for:—tune, pictures (by which I meant imagery), and a third, nameless quality I should now describe as an atmosphere of fantasy, which, for my taste at all events, could never be too wild.

Rossetti has said that poetry ought to be 'amusing', and I found it made the poem none the less amusing if I did not know exactly what it meant—or rather, what it 'said', for of course I did know what it meant to me. *The Raven*, for instance, meant that I was in a room—sombre, luxurious, hung with rich funereal wrappings and tapestries and curtains in black and purple—a room high up in a vast empty house, while just beyond the heavy door of carved and polished ebony was a silent landing—one of those dreadful landings I knew so well—flooded with a faint and ghastly light. It meant that somebody was wailing for a lost love—lost eternally, because gone to heaven, and nobody in this room would ever go to heaven, least of all that white-faced, black-clothed figure shrinking back in his chair, his eyes blazing with madness. The raven was no bird, no bird of ours, but a creature attracted out of the night by the call of this man's soul, which had awakened the whole house to a malevolent life that even now was drawing closer, pressing against the shut door.

That was the note: by which I mean it was the note of this particular poem, for I was happier really if terror were absent.

I shriek'd and leapt from my chair, and the orange roll'd out far,
The faint yellow juice oozed out like blood from a wizard's jar.

That, too, was the note. I even found it in such pieces as Tennyson's *Mariana*:

> *With blackest moss the flower-pots*
> *Were thickly crusted, one and all....*

(I give my old mistaken reading, because the flower-pots were an essential part of the picture it created.) But of Wordsworth's emotion recollected in tranquillity I had scant appreciation; still less was I susceptible to the charm of poems dealing with 'such topics as war, patriotism, prosperous love, religion, duty'—topics which I confess even to-day leave me cold.

Ulalume was my favourite poem, and it was indefinite enough to be inexhaustible. The music of the waxing and waning rhythm, the ominous beat of its repetitions, the gradual crescendo of a horror never actually named, the haunted beautiful landscape which I *knew*—these fascinated my imagination, which hovered round them, creating as much as it received. The magic was complex: it was partly in the tune, partly in the picture, partly in the extraordinary suggestiveness of certain words.

> *The skies they were ashen and sober;*
> *The leaves they were crispéd and sere—*
> *The leaves they were withering and sere;*
> *It was night in the lonesome October*

> *Of my most immemorial year;*
> *It was hard by the dim lake of Auber,*
> *In the misty mid region of Weir—*
> *It was down by the dark tarn of Auber,*
> *In the ghoul-haunted woodland of Weir.*

The dictionary meaning of many of the words I could not have given you—I certainly never looked them up in a dictionary—and yet their meaning in the poem was the same to me then as it is now.

But I found few complete poems of this kind: even to-day I should not be able to find many. A single line, sometimes even a single word, was sufficient to produce this peculiar effect, as of a drug acting not upon the senses but on the imagination. It was all quite unaccountable. Why should the famous lines, so elaborately suggestive in their intention—

> *Charm'd magic casements, opening on the foam*
> *Of perilous seas, in faery lands forlorn—*

have left me unmoved? What strange virtue was there in these:

> *Though the house give glimmering light,*
> *By the dead and drowsy fire. . . .*

A dozen simple words used every day in ordinary speech; yet they created a world deep and mysterious, into which I could gaze as into a dark glowing crystal, watching vision melt into vision.

Drowsy fires had indeed, then, as now, a runic charm for me.

> *Where glowing embers through the room*
> *Teach light to counterfeit a gloom,*
> *Far from all resort of mirth,*
> *Save the cricket on the hearth,*
> *Or the bellman's drowsy charm. . . .*

> *Good luck befriend thee, Son; for at thy birth*
> *The faery ladies danced upon the hearth.*
> *The drowsy nurse hath sworn she did them spy. . . .*

How vivid a picture those last lines called to life:—the firelight dancing on the shadowy wall, the child asleep in his bed, the quiet room, the old spectacled nurse nodding over her big book! Had they, indeed, some root that struck deep down into life, into a store of buried memories; was that drowsy nurse, after all, simply Emma?

'Hebrides' was another of my magic words.

> *Ah, by no wind are stirred those trees*
> *That palpitate like the chill seas*
> *Around the misty Hebrides!*

And 'trees' itself had a stirring of life in it, a stirring of the actual leaves.

In poetry it was what was *not* said, what was communicated secretly, as by the whispering of spirit to spirit, that I valued. I loved those lines that had no ending, that trailed on for ever into the infinite:

> *Following darkness like a dream....*

The words said nothing; I only knew that they entered into my mind, lulling it to a kind of quiescent state, a state of receptivity in which things came and went, a state which must have had all the semblance of extreme stupidity, since I was frequently aroused from it by a shake, accompanied by an exasperated comment on the vacancy of my expression.

And in truth I had not been thinking, though that was the excuse I would make. I did not begin to think till I began to talk, and I began to do both with a quite appreciable effort, just as if I were setting some kind of machinery in motion, which for a minute or two would not run quite smoothly.

And as sounds and words affected me, so, too, certain things in life would suddenly sweep through me in a flood of beauty, that seemed to fill my whole being, and reduce me to a state of paralysed immobility. I remember one such happening which took place during a holiday at the seaside. An arrangement had been made among us to meet at night on the beach and bathe in the moonlight. But on the night fixed for the adventure a white mist had rolled up out of the water, and the whole bay was shrouded by a thick veil, through which the splashing of the invisible waves sounded mysteriously. There was only a faint wash of palest gilt where the moon should have been. It was as if the entire earth had suddenly fallen under an enchantment, and coming out of the warm lighted house into this totally unexpected and unrecognizable world, I stood spellbound and solitary on the verge of it. I could hear voices and laughter. I could see the ghostly naked forms of the bathers appearing and disappearing as they passed in and out of the mist and splashed through the shallows; but I did not, could not, join them. It was unearthly, fantastic. Five yards from the shore nothing was visible; and out of this milky void a disembodied voice would float, or a small dream-like figure for a moment emerge. Presently the voices of uneasy mothers were added to these spirit voices, urging the more adventurous to return. Half laughing, yet fussy and anxious as hens, they hovered where the shore dipped down to the water's edge, counting their broods. One or two boys were missing, and eager cries called them to come back. It was a picture such as A. E. might have imagined and painted, but no painting could give the peculiar glamour of the reality. What had been designed as a mere frolic, had by some strange alchemy been transformed into a scene of radiant loveliness, a kind of spiritual blessing, like Wordsworth's field of daffodils.

But no; that is wrong; wrong for me, I mean; beauty rarely caused my heart to dance. Through all beauty there sounded for me a note of sadness. Though I loved it, it made me sad. If I wanted to dance and be happy I had to turn to games. Then I could forget, could enjoy the passing hour with the fullness of enjoyment; but beauty invariably awoke in me that old endless home-sickness, that old longing for a heaven that was not heaven, for an earth that was not earth, for a love that I knew I should never find either in heaven or on earth.

PART SIX

XVIII

It was during my last year at school that I began to write, moved by some impulse that had very little to do with literary ambition. I had no desire for publicity; journalism as a possible profession did not present itself to my mind. I knew a boy who had entered for several literary competitions organized by a popular weekly newspaper, but, though he eventually won a prize, and the successful piece was printed, it never occurred to me to try to follow his example. I had nothing whatever of the professional spirit: that point of view, that kind of writing, had no more interest for me than banking or engineering. Nor was it that I believed I had any particular talent, or that anybody would want to read what I should write. I wrote simply to express the other, secret life, without thought of anything else. I did not much care about anything else; by temperament I was as practical as one of the monks of the Thebaid.

I wrote badly, with a positive, not a negative, badness; for I had every fault except insincerity. What I was trying to make was a story, but I knew nothing about the construction of stories. In the opening chapter I merely described a boy as he sat in the same class-room where I myself, during detention, had been sitting when the idea first came to me. I did not try to present him objectively, nor yet did I think of him as myself, though I gave him all my own thoughts and emotions. I described the green beckoning branches of the elm-trees, visible through the open window; the soft breeze that entered with the sunlight, stirring the loose papers on the master's table and the old time-stained maps hanging on the wall; the voices, the sounds of ball and bat, that rose from the cricket field; the hot June sunshine on the yellow desks and forms, with their ink splashes, and roughly carved names. And all this was seen through a haze of my own vagrant fancies, memories, desires.

I worked over this first chapter very carefully, but when it was done decided to write the rest of the story without looking back till the whole should be finished. My aim remained unaltered; nor was it an unworthy one. It was that this book should reflect all the beauty I had found both in the real world and in my dream world. I saw this beauty as a river, flowing, flowing endlessly by me, while I stood lost in its dreamy enchantment upon the bank. I did not know that I might as well have tried to grasp an actual stream of water. In the eagerness of composition I was aware of no difficulty except that occasioned by the need to devise some kind of wooden bridge of story by which I could pass from scene to scene. The construction of these wooden bridges was dull work. I had a dim suspicion that I was scamping them and that they were of an extreme flimsiness and unsightliness, but I was perfectly happy again the moment I had passed them. It was all, in truth, less like writing than a form of daydreaming, in which I rebuilt the world after my own fashion—rebuilt it so that I could find a place there. And this was the secret of my pleasure, the source of my impulse, without which perhaps I should not have written a line. It was the pleasure of the exile who has returned to his native shore; the scenes I was describing so rapturously were not really the scenes I supposed them to be; they belonged to a country not marked on any map—that lost green island of the earlier years, which I could no longer visit in the old way.

Not that I was unhappy in exile. I knew my way about, and found it pleasant enough. I was always delighted to get back to school again after the holidays. And each year there was pleasanter than the last.

It was not a very big school. It consisted of some three hundred boys—all but a score or two of them day-boys—their ages varying from ten or eleven to seventeen or eighteen. And though I had many friends, and several who might have described themselves as chums, I had no really intimate friend. Intimate we were, of course, in a sense—that is to say, so far as the common ground upon which we met went. But it was always *their* ground, never mine; and everything connected with what appeared to me to be my more real life I had to keep hidden.

For there is nobody, perhaps, quite so conventional, in his own queer way, as the average schoolboy. I knew, for instance, that while it would be all right, and even meritorious, to point out the grosser passages in Chaucer (*The Wife of Bath's Prologue, The Reves Tale*), it would never do to say there was a poet called Rossetti who had written lovely things —*The Blessed Damozel, The Stream's Secret, My Sister's Sleep*. I made no such mistakes. I found life among this new set of boys as easy as I had found it among the old, being helped doubtless by the fact that one part of me fitted perfectly into the scheme of things as it was. My friends were of every kind —good, bad, and indifferent—including even a loutish youth, in some respects not unlike the traditional school bully, who on nearly my first day had pursued me into a remote corner of the playground with obviously bloodthirsty intentions, which had suddenly turned to extreme friendliness after he had gripped me by the shoulders and given me a shake or two. This surprising change of heart had been witnessed by another small boy, who presumed on it to approach nearer, was hailed with a sort of ogreish chuckle, and suffered such instant and outrageous punishment that in a way it was half comic.

I have never known anybody who approached so closely as this young giant did to one of those fabulous caprine beings in which man and beast are blended. He was slow of wit, brutal of nature, and, though seventeen, was in two or three of my classes. But he had the strength of a bull and I was rather proud of my relation with him, which was more or less that of a small and friendly Ulysses with a protective Polyphemus. He had enormous hands, and, spreading out and curving his fingers exactly the way a cat does his claws, he would drag them down the desk in front of him, tearing up the scored wood with his powerful nails, while his lips curled away from his white teeth. This performance fascinated me. I used to provoke him purposely in the security of the classroom for the sake of the thrill I got afterwards when he seized hold of me out in the passage, and whispered with a peculiar ferocity all the punishments I was about to suffer. Also it was pleasant to do what nobody else would have dared to do. Not that, on my part, much daring was required. I knew I was perfectly safe, because I knew that for some reason I had found favour in his eyes, and that my teasing secretly pleased him. He left, at the end of my first year, to become a sailor. . . .

The whole school was pervaded by a tone of slackness. Those who wanted to work, worked, but I was not one of them and there was no compulsion. In this my last year I had arranged my classes so that I had no home preparation at all, nor was the arrangement ever discovered. The principal masters were old, lethargic, drowsy. Nixon, the chief mathematical master, having chalked up a few questions on the blackboard, slumbered quite frankly through the remainder of the hour. All that was asked of you was that you should not disturb his sleep. If you did, he had a cane, and knew how to use it. Doctor Steen, the head, who taught Greek and Latin, was so blind that when a boy was sent to him in disgrace by one of the junior masters, all he had to do was to open the door softly and stand against the coat-rack—the Doctor would drone on without noticing him. Up here, in his room, on the broad window-seat, I sat with one or two others, looking down at the waiting cricket field, watching Henry Hull, the ancient porter, doddering about, listening to the subdued murmur from the town beyond, playing such games as could be played without noise. The construe was read openly from an English version: the questions were asked generally, so that two or three of the more industrious were deputed to answer for all. It was very peaceful, and nobody was ever punished. Those days, indeed, come back to me now faintly fragrant with what seems an old-world charm—they are like old letters one finds after long years hidden in a sachet.

I was conscious of that charm at the time: I was even

trying to get it—with its lazy, unexacting familiarity and sociability—into my story; which was to contain, for that matter, everything I had ever loved.

There was to be room found for the little country churchyard near Ballinderry, which I had discovered hidden away among fields and lanes, the church itself a grey old ruin. It was a neglected spot, and nature had half reconquered the ground, making of it a wild tangle through which the battered gravestones peeped. Yet some of the inscriptions were still decipherable, though a dark lichen had covered most of them. I had chanced on this graveyard quite unexpectedly one morning when out for a walk. The season was spring, but a spell of summer seemed to have fallen on this place: the winds were hushed, the air mild and caressing. And as I sat on a sun-warmed, fallen headstone, I felt that I had wandered into the very heart of Peace. Thrushes and rooks and starlings flitted about the church tower, while directly in front of me was a mass of flaming crimson blossom, where a flowering currant had found a root-hold among the crumbling stones. I know not what there was about this place that so entranced me. It was a beauty that seemed mingled with innocence and simplicity; it had a definitely *moral* quality, which dropped deep down into my soul and made me feel good. I very seldom felt good. I very seldom *was* good, though I loved goodness in other people. But as I sat in that churchyard all my restless thoughts and impulses sank away: I was like one of Wordsworth's little boys or little girls, and could have held a dialogue with the sage precisely in their manner had his mild old ghost come woolgathering by. . . .

There was the beauty of an autumn afternoon in the Ormeau Park at dusk, when, with the dead leaves thick on the deserted paths, I had sat listening to a German band playing somewhere out of sight beyond the railings. Through the twilight, with its yellow twinkling of street lamps, the music floated. The tune was the old *Lorelei*, but into the plaintive twang of those instruments all the melancholy of the earth had passed. It was as if the very soul of the empty park had found a voice, and were sobbing out its complaint to the November sky. . . .

There was the beauty of the Lagan Valley, filled with the sound of hidden running water, where the sluggish river plunged down through foaming weirs. A beauty, in summer, when the dark soil had burst into a pagan riot of growth, rich and green and luxuriant; but in winter desolate enough, suggestive of broken, unhappy loves, of last walks together, while the grey light gradually faded from the marsh-lands beyond the tow-path, and the trees stooped down over their own dark images. . . .

There was the beauty of the sea—an unearthly beauty, because it washed on the shores of my dream world. A strip of golden sand over which the dark blue water splashed in little creamy waves—thus it came back to me, forming always the same picture—a picture that more than any other was *my* picture. For, most of us, I suppose, have one picture that is somehow a part of our life, in which our life really takes place, and which is the last sight, perhaps, our dying eyes will see.

All this, and much else, I wished to introduce into my story; and all seemed bound up with the primary emotion upon which that story was based. I no longer dreamed as in the old days, but the memory of those dreams still haunted me, and I could not help seeking, if only in imagination, for my dream playmate. This book was a kind of attempt to bring him down to earth, to bring him into the world of my school life. It was composed in deepest secrecy: I had not the faintest intention of showing it to anybody: at the first sound of an approaching footstep I would hide my manuscript away and pretend to be doing something else. At last it was finished—on a tragic note—the note I felt instinctively every such story must reach if followed far enough. There remained nothing to do but to read what I had written—a goodly heap of manuscript. I turned back half nervously to the first page and began.

What had I expected? I do not know. But it was while I was reading, on this memorable evening, that for the first time I had experience of a strange phenomenon, for which I was then in no wise prepared, but to which I am now more or less resigned. On that night, however, it filled me with consternation; I could not understand what had happened. While I had been writing my tale it had been beautiful, moving, passionate (at all events, it had had these qualities for me), and now—now that it was written—it simply wasn't there. But where was it? I could have wept with disappointment. Where was my story? Who had robbed me of it and put in its place this feeble stilted rubbish, with its gushes of childish sentimentality? The first chapter remained just readable: hardly a sentence of the rest but racked my soul with torment. I made no attempt to patch it up. My fairy-gold was trash. This was the story I had written, but it was not the story I had tried to write, the story that had filled my mind while I *was* writing. It bore no resemblance to it. I had merely vulgarized and made trivial all I most deeply loved.

Presently I was able to examine it more calmly, but I could see not a sign of promise in it. Taken as mere writing, it was infinitely less competent than the work of the boy who had won a prize in *Answers*. It did not occur to me that I had been trying to do a vastly more difficult thing. Moreover, the thought, if I had had it, would have brought me no consolation, because unless I could do what I wanted to do I had no desire to do anything. And I was intelligent enough to see that what I had done was hopeless, that I couldn't write at all.

XIX

Let me at this point for a moment take a glance backward, though not very far backward, as far only as the winter that preceded the summer we have now reached, the winter during which I was confirmed. It is not an important date; my confirmation possessed for me not the slightest spiritual significance, was entirely a matter of form; but it did to some extent help me to realize where I stood in relation to the religion I was called on to accept. I was no longer a child; I had reached the age of puberty, with its momentous discovery of the sexual impulse as a kind of restless goad driving the herd of dream and waking thoughts into disquieting paths. For the first time I paused, as it were, and deliberately took stock of my position.

In these chapters there have been many references to a secret world, a secret life. I now tried to examine intellectually what had hitherto reached me almost entirely through imagination. Out of fragments of the world I shared with others, out of scattered glimpses of the past, out of nature, and out of my own dreams and desires, I had built up this world which I did not and could not share; though I believed that something very like it must at one time have existed, and even felt there might be just a chance that it existed still, in some inexplicable way. Its beginnings were bound up with the first dreams I ever dreamed; in its development it led me at last to that definite revolt from Christianity which was precipitated by, and which followed immediately on, my confirmation. It was not, as I have already said, so much that I disbelieved in the Christian creed (though I did now disbelieve in it) as that temperamentally I was antagonistic to this religion, to its doctrines, its theory of life, the shadow it cast across the earth. I was antagonistic at the very hour of my final initiation into its mysteries, which took place on an evening shortly before Christmas, in Saint Thomas's Church.

Yet by the ceremony itself I was not unmoved. The place, the music, the novelty of the whole experience, produced their effect upon me. The gallery, the remoter parts of the building, remained in obscurity; the lights shone upon the centre aisle and on the chancel. Demure maidens dressed in white sat on one side of this central aisle; the boys sat on the other; while fathers, mothers, elder sisters, and aunts looked on sentimentally from the pews behind. My own thoughts were more or less distracted by the fact that I was for the first time wearing a suit with long trousers, and this distracted mood prevailed even when the moment came for me to kneel before the altar and receive the episcopal blessing. But I enjoyed this moment, and I thought the bishop was hurrying unduly. I don't quite know what I wanted him to do. To pause dramatically, perhaps, when he reached me, and pronounce a special benediction. As it was, it was all over in a few seconds. 'Defend, O Lord, this thy Child with thy heavenly grace, that he may continue thine for ever, and daily increase in thy Holy Spirit more and more, until he come unto thy everlasting kingdom.' He had passed on to the next boy without a pause; it seemed to me he was simply racing through what was by far the most attractive part of the ceremony. The moment he had removed his hands from my head my interest in the scene died, and what had been designed as the beginning of my religious life proved to be the end of it. I was sick of this slavery to what were to me no more than empty conventions, sick of professing beliefs and desires which I did not feel; and on the very next Sunday I refused point-blank to go to church any more.

I refused obstinately. Neither punishments nor persuasions moved me. They had indeed, partly on account of the form they took, a hardening effect, so that I made up my mind definitely to lead from this on my own life in my own way.

Meanwhile, unguided, and more or less by chance, I had

stumbled on the poetry and religion and art of the Greeks, and in this discovery seemed to find what all along I had been seeking. I hung a print of a bust of Socrates on the wall of my bedroom, with another of the Hermes of Praxiteles; and these were to be my guardians, human and divine. But I had no learning; this paganism was a subjective thing, bearing no closer relation to reality than did my imagined Greece, which was merely a glorified reflection of my own countryside: while in my reading of Greek poetry and philosophy I was principally busy to find a confirmation of my private point of view. Certainly I seemed to find it—found an expression of thoughts and emotions and dreams that had haunted me from childhood. It was all, in truth, an emotion rather than a creed, reaching me through my senses much more than through my intellect. It was a paganism softened, orientalized, I dare say, to bring it into accord with what I desired; nevertheless, what appealed to me *was* to be found in the literature of Greece, and not elsewhere. The completed idea, the vision, was built up from the earlier dialogues of Plato, from the poets of the Palatine Anthology (Mackail's *Select Epigrams* having come by good fortune into my hands), from the fragments of Sappho, from Theocritus and the bucolic poets, from the Homeric Hymns, even from certain lyrical passages in the great dramatists. I have described it as orientalized, because a kind of romantic luxuriousness and sleepiness undoubtedly pervaded it. The landscape might be that of the world I knew best, but a hotter sun, the sun of Egypt or of Sicily, brooded upon it; and it was always summer, the summer of Theocritus, or of Giorgione's *Fête Champêtre*:

'Through the apple-boughs the sighing winds go softly, and from the quivering leaves sleep seems to drip.'

'The crests and hollows of the mountains are asleep, and the headlands and ravines, and the leaves, and all creeping things which the black earth nourishes, and the beasts of the mountains, and the race of bees, and the monsters in the depths of the dark-gleaming sea; and there is sleep among the tribes of broad-winged birds.'

Long before this, independently, I had arrived at the Greek view of nature. In wood and river and plant and animal and bird and insect it had seemed to me there was a spirit which was the same as my spirit. And here, in this poetry, every aspect of nature seemed to be perpetually passing into divinity, into the form and radiance of a god, while the human passed no less easily into tree or reed or flower. Adonis, Narcissus, Syrinx, Daphne—could I not see them with my own eyes? Could I not see Philomela flying low above the earth? Had I not, even in this land once blessed by Saint Patrick, caught a glimpse of that ill-mannered boy who, mocking the great Demeter while she drank, was straightway transformed into a lizard? The landscape was the landscape I loved best, a landscape proclaiming the vicinity of man, a landscape imbued with a human spirit that was yet somehow divine. 'At the birth of the nymphs', I read in the *Hymn to Aphrodite*, 'there sprang up pine-trees or tall-crested oaks on the fruitful earth, flourishing and fair. . . . But when the fate of death approaches, first do the trees wither on the ground, and the bark about them moulders, and the twigs fall down, and even as the trees perish so the soul of the nymph leaves the light of the sun.' It was a world in which either everything was spirit or nothing was: and it was young, there was a freshness even in the hottest sunshine.

'Sweet is the voice of the heifer, sweet her breath, sweet to lie beneath the sky in summer, by running water.'

It was this mixture of homeliness with something passionate and strange that made its beauty:

'As on the hills the shepherds trample the hyacinth underfoot, and the flower darkens on the ground.'

'Evening, you who gather all that bright morning scattered; you bring the sheep and the goat, the child back to his mother.'

A mysterious and deep understanding, it seemed to me, had existed in that far-off age between man and nature, and this understanding I shared to-day, or thought I shared. There were hours when I could pass *into* nature, and feel the grass growing, and float with the clouds through the transparent air; when I could hear the low breathing of the earth, when the colour and smell of it were so close to me that I seemed to lose consciousness of any separate existence. Then, one single emotion animated all things, one heart beat throughout the universe, and the mother and all her children were united.

In this poetry I found, too, my own sense of fellowship with every scaled and furred and feathered creature. There were modern poems written to the skylark or the nightingale, or to commemorate a favourite dog perhaps; but what modern poet would write of such tiny creatures as the ant or the grasshopper?

'Here beside the threshing-floor, O patient and toiling ant, I raise a memorial to you in this dry clod of earth, that the furrow and the corn of Demeter may charm you still, as you lie within your rustic tomb.'

The spirit of these poems was utterly different from the spirit of any modern poetry I had read. To the Greek, one bond united all mortal beings, their rights were equal, they shared the common life, for all there was the same uncertainty in the present, the same questionable future:

'Earth and Birth Goddess, thou who didst bear me and thou who coverest, farewell; I have accomplished the course between you and I go, not discerning whose or who I am, or whence I came to you.'

The voice of Tauros, the white dog of Melita, is 'prisoned in the silent pathways of night'. The 'poor partridge', slain by a cat, will never again ruffle his wings in the dawn: Earth is prayed to rest 'not lightly but heavily' upon him, lest his enemy drag out his remains. The shrill grasshopper 'drunk with dew' is not forgotten, though he no longer hides himself under the green leaves, 'sending forth a happy noise from his quick-fanning wings', but has been carried down to a dim lower world, to the 'dewy flowers of golden Persephone'. Somehow, to listen to his descendants whirring in the grass close by brought that old world in which he was so great a favourite very near to me. It was he who took up and prolonged the note when the string of the poet's lyre snapped, he whose evening hymn filled the house with pleasant noise, whose voice comforted the sleepless lover, whose song itself brought sleep. And the tame hare, and the favourite horse, and the swallow—all were remembered in words which had a simple gravity and affection that was no different from the affection one might feel for a child gone, too, on that same 'last road of Acheron'. One spirit, one fate, bound together all mortal children of the old Earth Mother; the lives of all were brief and perilous, their end sad and obscure. And when a voice passed into tree or plant, when the vine spoke, as in the poem of Evenus, it seemed to me in no way unnatural:

'Though thou devour me down to the roots, yet still will I bear so much fruit as will serve to pour libation on thee, O goat, when thou art sacrificed.'

It may be that the religious emotion is universal, finding an outlet, if not in this way, then in that; and it may be there was something of its rapture in my apprehension of nature. Certainly the Greek religions and cults and myths, of which I had so scanty and superficial a knowledge, probably misunderstanding a large part even of what I had read, were like a floating golden web that caught and held and coloured my imagination, though they had not, I dare say, really awakened what might positively be called faith. My deities were the Arcadian gods, the lesser gods, Pan and Hermes. The darker, more mystic element interwoven with the worship of Dionysos (the *truly* religious element, doubtless, with its blood-sacrifices and ecstasy, and mingled lust and madness), this was repellent to me because of the cruelty bound up with it. The deities I invoked, or evoked, were friendly, and more than half human; they were the deities of the poet and the sculptor:

'I who inherit the tossing mountain-forests of steep Cyllene, stand here guarding the pleasant playing fields, Hermes, to whom boys offer marjoram and hyacinth and fresh garlands of violets.'

And I was one of those boys, though I had been born into

a later age, when my offerings must be kept hidden. My gods were the protectors of the fields and orchards and flocks, who counselled the passing stranger where to rest at noon, and pointed out to him the clearest, coolest streams and wells from which to drink. Pan, who loved the rocks and woods, was associated in my mind with music, the music of leaves and running water and his own pipes; Hermes was a kind of divine playmate. These gods I loved because they had human limitations, were beautiful and strong and passionate, were neither solemn nor sad, and had morals not very different from my own. And though I somehow pictured Pan as rather old and Socratic; in spirit, in his sympathies, like Socrates, he too was young and loved to be with the young.

This adoration of youth was indeed one of the qualities of the Greek genius that most endeared it to me. I felt as I read their poetry what the Egyptian priest says in the *Timaeus*: 'O Solon, Solon, you Hellenes are never anything but children, and there is not an old man among you.... In mind you are all young.' And because I wanted so much these gods to be real, I felt that the earth would be almost empty without them. I would half shut my eyes, and peering through the green shadows of interlaced trees and brambles, under the streaming fire of the sun, would hypnotize myself into the belief that I could see them. And then, one day, it all very nearly came true.

It was June, and I was supposed to be working for an Intermediate examination, and had a book or two with me even on this blazing afternoon. It was hot and still. The breathless silence seemed unnatural; seemed, as I lay motionless in the tangled grass, like a bridge that reached straight back into the heart of some dim antiquity. I had a feeling of uneasiness, of unrest, though I lay so still—of longing and excitement and expectation: I had a feeling that some veil might be drawn away, that there might come to me something, some one, the Megistos Kouros perhaps, either with the winged feet of Hermes, or the thyrsus of Dionysos, or maybe only hairy-shanked Pan of the Goats. My state of mind just then was indistinguishable from that of the worshipper.

> Ἰώ, Μέγιστε Κοῦρε,
> Χαῖρέ μοι. . . .

I was certainly prepared to join in whatever rites or revels might be required. My body seemed preternaturally sensitive, my blood moved quickly, I had an extraordinary feeling of struggle, as if some power were struggling to reach me as I was trying to reach it, as if there *was* something there, something waiting, if only I could get through. At that moment I longed for a sign, some definite and direct response, with a longing that was a kind of prayer. And a strange thing happened. For though there was no wind, a little green leafy branch was snapped off from the tree above me, and fell to the ground at my hand. I drew my breath quickly; there was a drumming in my ears; I knew that the green woodland before me was going to split asunder, to swing back on either side like two great painted doors. . . . And then—then I hesitated, blundered, drew back, failed. The moment passed, was gone, and at first gradually, and then rapidly, I felt the world I had so nearly reached slipping from me, till at last there was all around me only a pleasant summer scene, through which, from the hidden river below, there rose the distant voices and laughter of a passing boating-party.

PART SEVEN

XX

The problem of 'what I was going to do' began to be discussed—principally when the whole family (except my eldest sister, who was now married) was gathered together at meal times. I hated these discussions; they filled me with embarrassment and humiliation by bringing home to me how superfluous I was. A friend of the wife of a London publisher had offered to use her influence to get me taken into the firm, and this was the only suggestion made that appealed to me. But my mother would not hear of it. Anything, it seemed, would be better than that I should live in London by myself. All I could say was to no purpose. To London I should not go. Even had she been assured that the most brilliant future awaited me there, I think it would have made no difference.

A brilliant future, however, was not in question: we were concerned merely with the problem of how I was to make a living; and since it seemed to me infinitely unlikely that there could exist anybody who would find my services worth paying for, I grew more and more despondent. My whole life, it now appeared to me, had been nothing but an elaborate preparation for failure. The one glimmering hope had been snuffed out with the London scheme. And a cloud of depression descended upon me, darkening my last days at school, while the months that followed were darker still. . . .

I had entered on the gloomiest period of my life, and I shall not dwell upon it. I was not at school; I had not yet been put to learn a trade. What malign spirit had taken possession of me I do not know, but each day seemed more dismal than the last. I became obsessed by the morbid idea that I was different from everybody else. The thought that I was growing older tormented me too. I wanted to be a boy always; I would have given gladly the remainder of my existence to have had the past five years over again. One day, while I was with my mother, buying a pair of boots, the shop assistant referred to me as a 'young man', and even this was enough to depress me for hours. I clung to the fact that I was not yet seventeen. My next birthday, I imagined, would separate me hopelessly and for ever from the past. The boys I had liked were turning into youths I detested—who oiled their hair, affected grown-up manners, and ran after girls. I became more and more solitary; and the happiness that ever more rarely visited me in dreams, turned, on awaking, to misery.

The temptation to put an end to it all began to haunt me. It seemed to me that the farther I advanced the deeper the gloom must grow. I had no experience to tell me that unhappiness, like happiness, has an end: I saw the present as eternal. So I hunted up ways of committing suicide—because I wanted to find a way that would be neither painful nor messy—and in the end decided to take laudanum.

I cannot make up my mind now as to whether I was really serious in this or not. I think probably not; but that whole period is strangely clouded and obscure. Without much trouble I obtained what, according to a Medical Dictionary, was a sufficient quantity of the drug, and once I had it in my possession I became indifferent. It was there, a last resource upon which at any time I could fall back; and there was no reason to act precipitately. Yet on the very next Sunday morning, while everybody was at church, I took the bottle from its hiding-place and mixed its contents with water in a tumbler. I felt no particular desire to drink it; the slightest thing would have made me throw it away. I was conscious of nothing but a general depression, through which any kind of positive action loomed as a temptation. And the moment after I had swallowed it was the first moderately cheerful one I had known for weeks. Instantly my apathy dropped from me in exciting speculations as to whether or not I should survive. I mean, in another life, for I had no doubt at all but that I had reached the end of this one. I was mistaken, however; my excitement speedily turned to nausea; I was violently sick, and from that relapsed into a state of coma. Yet I was sufficiently awake to be glad I had failed, and to know that I hadn't really wanted to die.

For two or three days I remained mysteriously ill. And when I recovered nothing had been altered by my experiment, a sickness of the soul still possessed me, a mortal loneliness. My mother noticed that all was not well. I assured her she was mistaken, but could not remove her suspicions. She insisted on my seeing a doctor, who put a stethoscope to various parts of my body, and finally wrote out a prescription —something to be taken after meals—with iron in it, I suppose, for I remember I took it through a glass tube. And my mother remained dissatisfied. She distrusted my recent habit of solitude, and kept urging me to go out with my friends, even after I had told her that I had no friends. This was true. In an incredibly brief time I had drifted away from everybody. I haunted the loneliest spots I could find; I buried myself in books; but human companionship was dearer to me than all the books in the world, and I seemed somehow to have been cut off from it permanently, as I had been cut off from my dream life.

XXI

Two of my brothers were in the linen business, but the linen business they considered to be overcrowded; another was in a bank, but there seemed to be little in favour of banking; so it was decided that I should be apprenticed to the tea trade. Nobody knew anything about the tea trade, and it was apparently on this singular ground that it was held to be suitable for me. I was taken by my brother-in-law to interview Henry Musgrave, the head of the firm, and on the following Monday morning started work at a salary of fifty pounds for five years.

As the Musgraves were among the wealthiest merchants in Belfast, these terms did not strike me as brilliant, nor was I surprised by the derision with which my eldest sister regarded my entrance into commercial life. Still, though generosity was not a Musgrave characteristic, I liked Henry: towards his brother, Edgar, when I watched him saving the backs of envelopes and lifting up little bits of string from the floor, my feeling was more one of curiosity. But things might have been worse. There were three other apprentices besides myself, two of whom I had known at school; and I liked the place; it was old-fashioned and very easy-going; not even a telephone had been installed.

My duties at first kept me a good deal in the open air, particularly round and about the docks, while during the mid-day interval, under the coaching of the manager, I learned the game of billiards. This, for some reason, did not meet with the approval of the boss of my own department, Robert Alexander (Mr. Robert, as he was always called); but since he knew very well in whose company I had been, nothing much could be said. And if they did little else for me, these new activities dissipated the cloud in which I had been living: my troubles disappeared; both physically and mentally I recovered my balance.

But of course I had been taken from school too soon—another year would have made all the difference. Perhaps my development had been slow; at any rate, now, when it was too late, there awoke in me an eagerness for learning which I had given no sign of possessing before, and I began to work at Greek, and also to make a systematic study of the Greek philosophers, aided by the monumental volumes of Zeller. In one of the upper lofts, in a recess near a dusty window, I rigged up a little den surrounded by a wall of tea chests, and to this solitude, shared only by an occasional mouse, I would vanish when opportunity arose. Here I kept my books, and here, when I was not wanted, I was allowed to read more or less in peace. Now and again Mr. Robert would pop his head round the corner and stand watching me and pulling his beard. 'Sonny, this is supposed to be a business establishment,' he would presently drawl. But he would end by taking up one of my books and turning its pages contemplatively, or by discussing for a few minutes *The Return of the Native*, which I had lent him, and which, though he was deeply interested in it, it took him a month to read.

I had not been in business very long before the manager advised me to turn my studies to a practical end. He assured me he was perfectly satisfied with the way I did my work; it was only that in case I *should* happen to have thought of another career he might as well tell me that the prospects in the tea trade were limited, and that unless one 'went on the road', or out to India or Ceylon, there were very few decently paid jobs, and he did not think I should be either happy or successful as a commercial traveller.

Not a word of this did I breathe at home. I knew there was no use talking about it, because to the tea trade I had been put, and to the tea trade I must stick—at all events for the present. If I reported what I had been told it would merely be regarded as a further proof of my unpracticality, and of the worry I seemed destined to create at every step.

So I continued as before, neither shirking my work nor, on the whole, disliking it. But in the tea trade itself I had no interest, because, apart from the money to be made out of it, it possessed none. To pretend that it took five years to learn it was simply a way of securing cheap labour. All there was to be learned could be learned in six months. The rest was a matter of office routine, and for this, too, a six months' training would have sufficed.

The chief life of the place centred in the mixing-room. It was in charge of the senior apprentice, and here—though the dry, dusty air was too solid for comfortable breathing—on the counter that ran under the windows I would sometimes sit watching the tea being tramped down into chests and half-chests, to an accompaniment of tales and songs. There was also now and then a game of cards, always of the simplest description. On these occasions a heap of empty packages, with their loose lids and hoops, would be propped against the door for the benefit of Mr. Robert. At a touch the whole pile would come tumbling down with a terrific clatter, at the same time effectually blocking up the entrance, so that before he could force his way in, and long before he had recovered his temper, the cards would have disappeared and work would be in full swing. This particular alarm signal (which never actually could be proved to be one) was the invention of James Quigley, who had been longer in the place than anybody else—except perhaps Mr. Robert himself—and who miraculously retained a reputation for an industry and handiness he may have possessed twenty or thirty years earlier. When I knew him he was as arrant and thirsty an old loafer as ever existed: nevertheless, he became my guide, philosopher, and friend.

Quigley was fond of conversation, was fond of young people, and was fond of giving me the benefit of his experience. My acquaintance with life seemed to him incomplete, though my curiosity was not unpromising; and he adopted the rôle of Mentor, being distinctly pleased, I fancy, to discover a Telemachus. Two of the other apprentices he described as 'mugs'; the third had outgrown the period of pupilage. So it was with Quigley I had my first drink—I mean, in the proper way, standing at the counter of a 'pub'— two drinks there were, because he was never a sponger: but from the backing of horses, his own favourite hobby, he warned me to keep clear. Quigley was completely unmoral, and completely without vice. He detested what he called 'meanness and greediness', but I never heard him condemn anything else. He unveiled certain of the pitfalls youth is apt to tumble into, taking it for granted I was of the kind that does tumble in (otherwise, I suppose, I should have been one of the 'mugs'); but his philosophy really was as ancient as the earth, and, though it was not expressed poetically, could all have been found in Herrick's poetry:

> *That Age is best, which is the first,*
> *When Youth and Blood are warmer....*
>
> *Then be not coy, but use your time....*

Such was its burden. It was the examples, however, rather than the precept, which interested me, for he liked to dwell upon the days when he himself had used his time. And I wronged him when I said he had no poetry, since there was surely poetry, of a kind, in those careless memories of opportunity grasped, those adventures of a light-hearted and very unspiritual lover. Perhaps it was because the adventures had all happened in mellow, golden years long before I was born; because the other persons involved were now either grandmothers or it may be but a little heap of silvery bones in some quiet old churchyard; or because of their rural setting (for as a youth he had lived in the country), that they appealed to me. At all events, those tales of summer lanes, and leafy copses, and shadowy barns with the corn piled high, created in my mind pictures that were like the pictures of a rougher and homelier Theocritus.... 'Ah, once again may I plant the great fan on her corn-heap, while she stands smiling by, with sheaves and poppies in her hands....'

When I knew Quigley he was an old white-haired, white-bearded man, bordering on seventy; but so perfect had been his physique that he was still powerful and good to look at, without a trace either of the feebleness or grossness of age. He was a pagan who had never heard of paganism: his mind was simple and earthy, entirely unspiritual, and entirely free from corruption.

> *Gather ye Rose-buds while ye may,*

for

> *Golden lads and girls all must,*
> *As chimney-sweepers, come to dust.*

That was the wisdom he tried to teach me, with many details concerning the gathering, and many descriptions of the roses. His own songs you will find neither in the pages of Herrick nor of Shakespeare, but they were entirely free from that taint of music-hall vulgarity which characterized the songs of the younger men. And he frequently sang while I sat and watched him at work, hooping the chests with their slender willow bands, hammering in one nail, perhaps, between every other verse. I can remember the tunes of these songs perfectly, but only fragments of their words. Here is the beginning of one of them:

> *Patsy McGann, you must marry my daughter,*
> *Patsy McGann, my child you must wed;*
> *Five golden sovereigns, Patsy, I'll give you,*
> *And the brass warming-pan, and the old feather-bed.*

And this, which was sung with a great flourishing of the hammer:

> *O, I'm ninety-five, I'm ninety-five,*
> *And to live single I'll contrive.*

In a less defiant key were the verses of

> *When I was a wee thin'*
> *I lived with my granny,*
> *And many's the caution*
> *The ould woman give me;*

> *She bid me be wise*
> > *And take care of the boys*
> *And not let my dimity*
> > *Over my knee.*

But again the gayer note was struck by a very long song, which, from both tune and words, was evidently designed to be sung in a tavern, and to a company well supplied with beer and tobacco:

> *O, there was three flies*
> *Upon a time*
> *Resolved to travel*
> *And to change their clime;*
> *The one was green*
> *And the one was blue*
> *And the other one was*
> *A yeller one too:*
> *So off they flew*
> *With a merry merry hum*
> *And they told their mammas*
> *For to. . . .*

The rest, I suppose, would be considered coarse, though neither in it nor the others was there a hint of nastiness. Nor was I myself of a squeamish habit of mind, so that, one and all, they bring back to me principally the summer afternoons when I so often heard them sung, with the sun slanting through the open windows across the dusty floor, the throb of the old gas-engine that worked the hoist faint in the distance, the venturesome mouse (which I thought of as a lady mouse) who would peep out at us with bright black little eyes, and then delicately approach and daintily drink up two or three of the tobacco spittles she found so delicious in this dusty waterless world.

When one thinks of the incalculable difference a little leisure makes in life, it seems strange that anybody should wish to adopt American habits of 'hustle' and 'rush'. The time of which I write is not after all so very long ago, and yet I am sure that to-day you could not find a business house conducted as this one was. And it was prosperous. Things, doubtless, were not squeezed quite so dry as they might have been; but when one's life, or the greater part of it, is passed in certain fixed conditions, is not the pleasantness of those conditions more important than the distinction of paying a super-tax? If I had been chained all day long to a desk I should have been unhappy: as it was, I was happy, my mental growth was not checked; on the contrary, my mind expanded more rapidly and freely than it had ever done before; I did not acquire elderly and methodical habits; the spirit of boyhood was left untouched. I had been brought into contact with ordinary rough-and-tumble life, but I had not been caught in the wheels of a machine.

XXII

I had been at work for only a very few months when a new apprentice came. It was my business to teach him his duties, and on a cold bright winter morning, when the ground was white with frost and a thin powder of snow, we set off for the docks. In the still, grey water the boats, looking strangely naked and black, were reflected as in a glass. Gulls wheeled restlessly about the masts and funnels; the wintry sun shone on frozen ropes and slippery decks; the ground rang with a hard metallic sound. Crates and bales, boxes and sacks were being piled on the wharves; iron trucks were busy, for the dock-labourers were working hard to keep themselves warm, their faces, ears, and hands scarlet, their breath turning to vapour the moment it passed their lips.

I had always found this scene attractive, and, though it was by now familiar enough, and I knew these boats were, with one or two rare exceptions, merely cross-channel steamers and coasters, it still continued to suggest romance, the great unexplored world that lay beyond my experience, glimmering with a mysterious fascination. To-day there was added to this the pleasure of acting as guide to my companion, of showing him *our* boats, *our* sheds, of telling him what he must do, of introducing him to the different shipping clerks. And through it all I was becoming more and more conscious of something pleasanter still, of an uplifting of the spirit that turned everything to beauty and filled my mind with sunlight. I knew this sunlight well, because it was the sunlight of my dream world. A long time had gone by since it had last shone for me, but with its first rays it burned up the intervening period like a thin sheet of paper, and filled me with a peculiar exultation. I seemed to be approaching a point; we both seemed, actually, physically, with every step we took, to be drawing nearer to a point where the wide sea flowing between my two worlds was narrowed to a stream one might pass dry-shod: my conduct of the business we were engaged on grew more and more mechanical.

Meanwhile the new boy walked beside me, rather shy, and with a simple, unconscious charm about him that I had felt from the moment (an hour or two back) when he had been introduced to me by his father. I prolonged our walk unnecessarily: I did not want to go back at all. . . .

And thus began a friendship which as the days passed, and then the weeks and the months, grew ever closer and deeper, till at last it seemed to draw into itself the two divergent streams of my life, so that for the first time, in dreaming and waking, they found a single channel. Somehow, somewhere, I felt that a shadow had been lifted. It was as if in my spirit a new day were breaking, transforming everything in the world around me, because I saw everything now in its fresh clear light.

When I was with this boy I was happy, and I could conceive of no greater happiness than to be with him always. He was an odd enough youngster in his ways, not a bit like any other boy I had known; but he was extraordinarily lovable. Sometimes, indeed, the sunshine, filled with little dancing golden dust specks, touching his hair or his cheek, would set me dreaming of him as a kind of angel who had strayed into this world by chance, or perhaps not quite by chance. The pleasantness of his manner, of his temper; his kindness, his intelligence, a sort of childish quality there was in his gaiety—all helped to deepen the affection I had for him. The future lay before us like a wide green plain. There were plans and day-dreams—plans that involved leaving our present employment and going to a university. Life in this humdrum old warehouse, amid its simple daily tasks, amid its comings and goings, its working hours and hours of leisure, became a wonderful voyage of discovery to be undertaken no longer alone.

Both here, and at home after the day's work was finished, we were constantly together. I showed him my writings, I got him to read poetry, to listen to music; I poured out all my enthusiasms, and in return became absorbed in his. That they took me into the unfamiliar paths of scientific theory and experiment did not matter. I read books on astronomy, and geology, and physics; he tried to interest me in mathematics, and of all our studies this was the only one I was obliged to abandon. But if I could make no headway here, we splashed happily enough in the shallows of philosophy, and it was while we were reading Caird's *Evolution of Religion* that between his father and mother a momentous discussion took place (of which I heard nothing until years later) as to whether this friendship should be discouraged or allowed to continue. They had been extremely kind to me, asking me frequently to the house; but they were very strict in their attitude to religion, and it was because of the Caird book and of Spencer's *First Principles*, which were supposed to have been my choice, that the discussion arose. In the end (I cannot help thinking it was his mother's counsel that prevailed) they decided not to interfere, but to let things take their course. . . .

I have wandered too far into the future in all this—farther than the scheme of these pages really carries me. For I see them, somehow, as embracing a definite period, which began in dreamland and ended with the winter morning of this chapter's opening. Or perhaps I should say that it ends on an evening some five or six months later.

I had never spoken of the affection which now filled my life: I had never alluded to it, though I had often longed to do so, though I had even once or twice tried to do so, though I knew it must for ever remain incomplete unless I did do so. Incomplete, that is, for me: for the rest I did not, could not know. And thus it went on, until I thought of a way by which I might surmount my shyness, or at least circumvent it—a way which would at any rate be easier than speech.

For some months back I had been keeping a diary, or journal, writing in it not regularly, but still fairly frequently. I wrote just before going to bed, and I poured out everything

I felt, for I intended to destroy it (and did do so) when the book should be filled. What I wrote was not meant to be read. I wrote as the servant of King Midas whispered into the hollow earth. Yet now I wanted him to read it. I knew it contained pages he might find bewildering, extravagant, and perhaps distasteful: but I also knew that if I looked back over it with a view to tearing out such pages I should never show it at all.

And the desire to take him completely into my confidence had begun to haunt me. It was what filled my mind as we walked home together one day some five or six months after our first meeting, and what kept me silent when, later on, we went out for a ramble through the fields and woods by the Lagan. Yet, though I was silent, I was intensely excited, for I had made up my mind to conquer my cowardice. Already I had had an opportunity to do so, and had put it off by coming out here. I would put it off no longer.

'There is something I have at home which I want to show you—something I have written. Do you mind turning back?'

Without questioning me he did what I asked.

And when once more we had reached the house in Mount Charles I took him upstairs to the room I now used as a study, and where I knew we should not be disturbed. It was growing dusk, but I welcomed the minutes I could employ on busying myself with the lamp, and fumbled longer than was necessary as I unlocked the desk where was my manuscript book. I gave him the book, moved the lamp over near to an arm-chair, and myself sat down at the table, some distance off, and facing the window. For the first time I had admitted someone to my secret world, to my innermost thoughts. . . .

Already he must have crossed the threshold. In the quiet of the room I could hear no sound except now and then the rustle of a page when he turned it. For an instant I glanced at him. His face was a little flushed, his dark hair tumbled down over his forehead. But I turned away quickly and did not look back. I sat waiting, trying now to shut out every thought from my mind. . . .

The time slowly drew on: half an hour, nearly an hour must have gone by. The window grew darker and darker, and presently I knew that in a little, a very little while, the reading must come to an end. Then the silence seemed all at once to grow so intense that I felt nothing could ever again break it.

November 1923.
April 1925.

Printed in Great Britain
by Amazon

APOSTATE